## THE LIBRARY OF TRADITIONAL WISDOM

The Library of Traditional Wisdom has as its aim to present a series of works founded on Tradition, this term being defined as the transmission, over time, of permanent and universal truths, whose written sources are the revealed Scriptures as well as the writings of great spiritual masters.

This series is thus dedicated to the *Sophia Perennis* or *Religio Perennis* which is the timeless metaphysical truth underlying the diverse religions, together with its essential methodological consequences.

It is in the light of the *Sophia Perennis,* which views every religion "from within," that may be found the keys for an adequate understanding which, joined to the sense of the sacred, alone can safeguard the irreplaceable values and genuine spiritual possibilities of the great religions.

# The Play
## of
# Masks

# FRITHJOF
# SCHUON

WORLD WISDOM BOOKS INC.

© 1992 by Frithjof Schuon

Translated from the French

Published in French as
*Le jeu des masques*
Lausanne, Switzerland
1992

Library of Congress Cataloging-in-Publication Data

Schuon, Frithjof, 1907-
  [Jeu des masques. English]
  The play of masks / Frithjof Schuon.
     p.  cm.—(The Library of traditional wisdom)
  Translation of: Le jeu des masques.
  Includes bibliographical references and index.
  ISBN 0-941532-14-3 : $9.00
  1. Metaphysics.  2. God.  3. Religion—Philosophy  4. Ontology  I. Title.
II. Series
BD112.S21513   1991
291.2—dc20                                    91-18219

Printed on acid-free paper in The United States of America

For information address World Wisdom Books, Inc.
P. O. Box 2682, Bloomington, Indiana 47402-2682

# Contents

# Foreword

Like most of our books, this new volume is not dedicated to one clearly delimited subject, but rather represents a general survey; the chapters are small independent treatises which often summarize the entire doctrine. The third article of this collection has given its name to the whole book; coincidentally, this title is well suited to a dialectic which presents the same fundamental theses in diverse aspects, repeated out of concern for clarity as much as for completeness.

Without a doubt, metaphysics aims in the first place at the comprehension of the whole Universe, which extends from the Divine Order to the terrestrial contingencies — this is the reciprocity between *Ātmā* and *Māyā* — yet it offers in addition intellectually less demanding but humanly crucial openings; which is all the more important in that we live in a world wherein the abuse of intelligence replaces wisdom.

Even if our writings had on the average no other result than the restitution, for some, of the saving barque that is prayer, we would owe it to God to consider ourselves profoundly satisfied.

# Prerogatives of the Human State

Total intelligence, free will, sentiment capable of disinterestedness: these are the prerogatives that place man at the summit of terrestrial creatures. Being total, the intelligence takes cognizance of all that is, in the world of principles as well as in that of phenomena; being free, the will may choose even that which is contrary to immediate interest or to what is agreeable; being disinterested, sentiment is capable of looking at itself from without, just as it can put itself in another's place. Every man can do so in principle, whereas animals cannot, a fact which cuts short the objection that not all men are humble and charitable; no doubt, the effects of the "Fall" weaken the prerogatives of human nature, but they cannot abolish them without abolishing man himself. To say that man is endowed with sentiment capable of objectivity means that he possesses a subjectivity not closed in on itself, but open unto others and unto Heaven; in fact, every normal man may find himself in a situation where he will spontaneously manifest the human capacity for compassion or generosity, and every man is endowed, in his substance, with what could be called the "religious instinct."

Total intelligence, free will, disinterested sentiment; and consequently: to know the True, to will the Good, to love the Beautiful. "Horizontally," the Truth concerns the cosmic, hence phenomenal, order; "vertically," it concerns the metaphysical, hence principial, order. And likewise with the Good: on the one hand, it is practical, secondary, con-

1

tingent; on the other, it is spiritual, essential, absolute. Similarly again with Beauty, which at first sight is outward, and it is then the aesthetic quality, that of virgin nature, of creatures, sacred art, traditional crafts; but with greater reason is it inward, and it is then the moral quality, nobleness of character. According to an Islamic saying, "God is beautiful and He loves Beauty"; which means implicitly that God invites us to participate in His Nature — in the Sovereign Good — through Virtue, in the context of the Truth and the Way.

Ideally, normatively and vocationally, man is Intelligence, Strength and Virtue; now, it is important to consider Virtue in two aspects, one "terrestrial" and the other "celestial." Socially, it demands humility and compassion; spiritually, it consists of fear and love of God. Fear implies resignation to the Divine Will; love implies trust in Mercy.

What is fear and love towards God becomes — mutatis mutandis — respect and good will towards the neighbor; good will as a matter of principle towards any stranger, not weakness towards someone known to be unworthy. Love implies fear, for one can love only what one respects; trust in Divine Mercy and mystical intimacy with Heaven indeed allow of no casualness; this also follows from that crucial quality which is the sense of the sacred, wherein fear and love meet.

In the experience of the aesthetic and of the erotic, the ego is extinguished — or forgets itself — before a grandeur other than itself: to love a reality worthy of being loved is an attitude of objectivity that the subjective experience of fascination cannot abolish. This is to say that love has two poles, one subjective, the other objective; it is the latter that must determine the experience since it is the reason for being of the attraction. Sincere love is not a roundabout way of loving oneself; it is founded upon an object worthy of admiration, of adoration, of desire for union; and the quintessence of every love, and even of every virtue, can only be the love of God.

\*

\*  \*

The complexity of our subject allows us to consider it now from another angle and to take account of other points of reference, and this at the risk of repetition, which cannot be avoided in such a matter.

Human intelligence is, virtually and vocationally, the certitude of the Absolute. The idea of the Absolute implies on the one hand that of the relative and on the other that of the relationships between the two, namely the prefiguration of the relative in the Absolute and the projection of the Absolute in the relative; the first relationship gives rise to the personal God, and the second, to the supreme Angel.[1]

Human will is, virtually and vocationally, the tendency towards the absolute Good; secondary goods, whether they be necessary or simply useful, are determined indirectly by the choice of the supreme Good. The will is instrumental, not inspirational: we know and love, not what we will, but rather we will what we know and love; it is not the will that determines our personality, it is intelligence and sentiment.[2]

Human sentiment — the soul if one wishes — is, virtually and vocationally, love of the Sovereign Beauty and of its reverberations in the world and in ourselves; in the latter case, the beauties are virtues and also, on a less eminent plane, artistic gifts. "God," "myself," "others": these are three dimensions to which correspond respectively piety, humility and charity or, we could say, the contemplative, characterial and social qualities.

In the case of piety — which is essentially the sense of the sacred, of the transcendent, of profundity — the complementary virtues of humility and charity are directed towards the Sovereign Good and make It their object; which is to say

1. This angel is the *Metatron* of the Kabbalah, the *Rūḥ* of the Koran and the *Buddhi* — or *Trimūrti* — of the *Vedānta;* it is also the Holy Ghost of Christian doctrine in its function of illuminating hearts.

2. The words "sentiment" and "sentimental" too often evoke the idea of an opposition to reason and the reasonable, which is abusive since a sentiment can be right just as a reasoning can be wrong.

that the quality of piety coincides in the end with holiness, which implies, a priori, joy through God and peace in Him. In this context, humility becomes awareness of our metaphysical nothingness, and charity becomes awareness of the divine immanence in beings and in things; to have a sense of the sacred is to be aware that all qualities or values not only proceed from the Infinite but also attract towards It. The soul, we have said, is quintessentially love of the Sovereign Beauty; from a less fundamental and more empirical point of view, we could say that the substance of the soul is the unconscious search for a lost Paradise, which in reality is "within you."

If the fundamental virtues are beauties, conversely each sensible beauty bears witness to the virtues: it is "pious" — that is "ascendent" or "essentializing" — because it manifests celestial archetypes; it is "humble" because it submits to the universal laws and, because of this, excludes all excess; and it is "charitable" in the sense that it radiates and enriches without ever asking for anything in return.

Let us add that in the human world, spirituality alone engenders beauty, without which the normal and non-perverted man cannot live.

\*

\* \*

The rigorous virtues, such as courage and incorruptibility, are on the one hand linked indirectly to the fundamental virtues and on the other are explained by the fact that we live in a limited and dissonant world; in Paradise, the aggressive and defensive virtues no longer have any reason for being. To fight for a just cause is to be charitable towards society; and to affirm towards men an authority that belongs to us by divine right is to be humble towards God. It is thus that every virtue, be it combative or adamantine, is connected directly or indirectly with the love of God, otherwise it could not be a virtue, precisely.

If piety, humility and charity are the greatest virtues, impiety,[3] pride, egoism and malice, will be the greatest vices; this is only too evident, but it is worth specifying this, all the more so since it is sometimes less difficult to fight a concrete fault than to realize an ideal of virtue. Beside the vices, there are also the caricatures of virtue, which being stupid or hypocritical are vicious in their turn: since impiety, pride and egoism are defects, it does not follow that false piety, false humility and false charity are qualities. Unquestionably, goodness is integral only on condition of being combined with strength.[4]

Besides virtue — spontaneous beauty of soul — there is also the effort towards virtue; the two moreover are in most cases combined. Doubtless, an attitude or a behavior that one must force oneself to practice is not yet an established virtue, even though it is already a kind of virtue if the intention is sincere.

*

\* \*

Our personality is founded upon that which we know to be real, and consequently also, but in a negative sense, upon that which we know to be unreal, or less real.

Similarly, our personality is founded upon that which we will, namely a given good and with all the more reason the good as such, and consequently also upon that which we reject, namely a given evil and a fortiori evil as such.

Similarly again, our personality is founded upon that which we love, namely beauty — be it physical, moral or

3. By impiety we mean, not the mere fact of not believing in God, but the fundamental tendency not to believe in Him; herein lies the whole difference between the "accident" and the "substance."

4. A Russian monk told us that Jesus treated the Temple merchants harshly in order to show that He was capable of exercising violence — an opinion which, when properly understood, is not lacking in pertinence, despite its paradoxical and unseemly aspect.

archetypal — and consequently also, in a negative sense, upon that which we detest, namely ugliness in all its aspects. A remark may be called for here: clearly, the beauty of a morally ugly person obliges us neither to love this person because of his beauty, nor to deny this beauty because of his moral ugliness; inversely, the ugliness of a morally beautiful person obliges us neither to detest this person because of his ugliness, nor to deny this ugliness because of his moral beauty. Confusions of this kind frequently occur on planes more subtle than the one at issue here, so that it is worth taking the trouble to point out these abuses of judgement.

Beauty is the substance, and ugliness the accident; the relationship is the same between love and hate; it is the relationship between good and evil in an altogether general sense. The world is fundamentally made of beauty, not ugliness, and the soul is made of love, not hatred; the world could not contain any ugliness if it did not contain a priori far more beauty,[5] and we have a right to aversion only by reason of the greatness of our love.

To discern the real is also to discern the unreal, or the less real, the contingent, the relative; to will the good is by that very fact to reject evil; to love the beautiful is ipso facto to detest the ugly, be it only through absence of love or through indifference. For we find ourselves in a world woven of imperfections, which obliges us to perceive its limitations and dissonances and to reject or combat them if need be.

\*

\* \*

We could also say that intelligence — according to whether it is applied to the Absolute or the contingent, to the Real or the illusory — is either unitive or separative: when unitive, it assimilates; when separative, it eliminates.

---

5. At least in normal circumstances, which predominate by far over the exceptional conditions of the "Iron Age."

Nevertheless the essence of intelligence can only be union, namely synthesis, not analysis, or contemplation, not discrimination.

Likewise, the will, according to whether it seeks the good or opposes evil, is either positive or negative — leaving aside the human possibility of inverting the normal order of things: when positive, the will is constructive, it actualizes or creates; when negative, it rejects or destroys. But the essence of the will is the choice of the good and the actualization of this choice; all secondary volitions derive from this according to the circumstantial contingencies imposed by the here-below, and which could not exist close to God.

Likewise again, sentiment, according to whether it reacts to the true or the false, to good or evil, to the beautiful or the ugly — and this apart from the question of knowing whether or not the reaction is appropriate — is either attraction or aversion, either love or hatred: the desire for union or on the contrary, the desire to turn away. The essence of sentiment is nonetheless love, because the essence of the Real is beauty, goodness, beatitude.

Hatred, when it is directed against people or against good things, harms humility and charity as much as it does piety; scorn, however, may be a self-defensive reflex; if physical disgust is permissible, moral disgust is so with all the more reason. Passional hatred also injures intelligence since it violates truth; it is not for nothing that one speaks of "blind hatred." But there is a hatred which on the contrary is lucid and thus has nothing passional about it, and this is the aversion to our own faults and to what corresponds to them in the world around us.

Intelligence should operate in virtue of an assessment, not out of a sentimental reaction; the will, by contrast, may operate in both ways, on condition that the option be appropriate. To ask what the purpose of sentiment is, is to ask what the purpose of love is: now, like knowledge, love seeks union, with the difference that in the first case the union is intellective and in the second, affective; in Hindu terms, this is the difference between *jnāna* and *bhakti*.

In a world largely under the influence of the centrifugal principle — the *princeps hujus mundi* — union and love cannot avoid being accompanied by a negative mode; ambiguity enters into the very definition of *Māyā*, the Absolute alone being beyond oppositions. Thus there is no contradiction in the fact that sentiment, while coinciding substantially with love, nonetheless implies the possibility of aversion.

To be beyond oppositions means: beyond modes and accidents, such as activity and passivity, the dynamic and the static, hot and cold, white and black; or beyond opposite excesses, such as agitation and indolence, or violence and weakness; but it cannot mean: beyond the true and the false, or good and evil, for in these cases the second term is a privation of being, if it may be so expressed, and not a mode of manifestation.

\*

\* \*

A metaphysical digression might be relevant here. To the attestation that *"Brahman* is Reality" *(Brahman satyam)* is joined the information that "the world is merely appearance" *(jagan-mithyā);* similarly — in an altogether different traditional climate — the axiom that "God alone is" *(illā 'Llāh)* requires as its negative complement the idea that "there is no other divinity" *(lā ilāha).* But this negation is compensated, on its own ground as it were, by the basically immanentist affirmation that "Muhammad is the Messenger of God" *(Muḥammadun rasūlu 'Llāh),* which in the present context means that "the Perfect is the emanation of the Principle"; in an analogous way, the Vedantic idea that "the world is merely appearance" is compensated by its positive complement, the idea that "the soul is not different from *Brahman" (jivo brahmaiva nāparah).*

8

In the doctrinal message of Islam as well as in the Hindu message, the affirmation of transcendence is defined extrinsically by means of a relativizing negative affirmation, which in its turn is surpassed by a compensatory affirmation of immanence. According to transcendence, we are supposed to love only the Sovereign Good, to which our power of love is proportioned since we are men; according to immanence, "it is not for the love of the spouse that the spouse is dear, but for the love of *Ātmā* which is in him."

When speaking of specifically human intelligence, one can proceed from the notions of transcendence and immanence; in other words, the essential question is that of knowing, on the one hand, what the loftiest content of the spirit is, and on the other, what its deepest substance is. The answer is furnished — in Western modality — by the Eckhartian concepts of the superontological, hence transpersonal, "Divinity" *(Gottheit)* and the "uncreate Intellect" *(aliquid . . . increatum et increabile).* From this may be deduced the following definition: integral and primordial man is the Intellect and the consciousness of the Absolute. Or again: man is faith and the idea of God; immanent Holy Spirit on the one hand, and transcendent truth on the other.

*

* *

According to an initial and synthetic logic, we would say that the intelligence aims at the true, the will at the good, and love at the beautiful. But in order to ward off certain objections, we must specify that the intelligence is made to know all that is knowable and consequently has as its object also the good and the beautiful and not only the true; similarly, the will aims at all that deserves to be willed, thus also at the beautiful and the good; love in its turn aims at all that is lovable, thus also at the true and the good. In other words: from the standpoint of intelligence, the good and the beautiful are quite clearly truths, or let us say realities; from the standpoint of the will, the true and beauty are goods;

and from the standpoint of love, the truth and the good have their beauty, which is much more than a manner of speaking.

*

\* \*

Intelligence and will when taken together constitute what we may call the "capability" of the individual, whatever his moral and aesthetic sensibility may be.

Similarly, sensibility and will when taken together constitute the "character" of the individual, whatever his intelligence may be.

And again, intelligence and sensibility when taken together constitute the "scope" of the individual, whatever his strength of will may be.

Thus, administrative qualification, organizational skill and strategy pertain to the psychological dimension we call "capability," rather than to intelligence or will alone; courage and incorruptibility pertain to "character" rather than to will or sensibility alone; the powerful profundity of great poets pertains to "scope," not to sensibility or intelligence alone. All these gifts have a conditional, but not an unconditional, value: in Paradise one no longer has need of skill, because there is no longer anything to organize; neither does one need courage, because there is no longer any evil to combat; and one no longer has need of genius, because there is no longer anything to invent or produce. On the other hand, one cannot do without the essential virtues — piety, humility and charity — for they pertain to the very nature of the Sovereign Good, which is to say that they are part of our being.

Truth, Way and Virtue; Virtue is the touchstone of our sincerity; without it, Truth does not belong to us and the Way eludes us.[6] The Truth is what we must know; the Way is what

---

6. "Though I speak with the tongues of men and of angels, and have not charity, I am become as sounding brass, or a tinkling cymbal." I Cor. 13:1.

we must do; Virtue is what we must love, become and be. The sufficient reason for the three fundamental perfections of man is the consciousness of the Absolute; without the possibility of this consciousness, the prerogatives of the human state would be unaccountable.

Truth, Way, Virtue; in other words: doctrine, method, qualification; discriminative and contemplative intelligence, realizatory will — at once forceful and persevering — and soul capable of objectivity, hence of disinterestedness, compassion, generosity. From the more particular point of view of spiritual alchemy it could be said: meditative comprehension, operative concentration, psychic conformity; this third element means that illuminating comprehension and transforming concentration require a climate of moral beauty. Whosoever says beauty, says goodness and happiness, or beatitude; which allows us to paraphrase the well-known Platonic formula thus: "Goodness — and with it beatitude — is the splendor of the true."

\*

\*  \*

Besides his objective intelligence, free will and capacity for disinterestedness, the human being is distinguished by thought and language, and as to his bodily form, by the vertical position; memory, imagination and intuition he has in common with animals. Reason, however, belongs to man only; we say reason and not intelligence, for on the one hand intelligence cannot be reduced to reason, and on the other, it is also to be found in the animal kingdom. Incontestably, animals also possess will and sentiment; the difference between them and men is absolute and at the same time relative: it is absolute with respect to the specifically human prerogatives, and relative with respect to the faculties as such.

As regards reason, theologians rightly consider that it is a sort of infirmity due to the "Fall" of Adam, and that the angels do not possess it since they are invested with the direct perception of principles, causes and effects. Nonetheless, reason has to have a positive aspect, in the sense that it is inseparable from language and that it can coexist with angelic intuition, or — what amounts to the same thing — with intellectual intuition, or pure intellection. As for articulated thought, even the angels have to be able to make use of the rational faculty, otherwise there would be no sacred scriptures. When all is said and done, reason becomes an infirmity only in the case of abusive speculation by the ignoramus who pretends to knowledge. An angel or a sage can certainly be rational, but never rationalistic; he need not "conclude" when he can "perceive," but he may explain an intellective perception with the aid of a dialectic which is perforce that of the logician.

The fact that the animals — like the angels — have intuition but not reason gives rise to the curious phenomenon of zoolatry, more especially as in them horizontal intuition is often more developed than in men, so that they appear like traces of celestial archetypes, or like their "mediums" so to speak. It may be noted that there are animals sensitive to spiritual influences, so much so that they are able to vehicle them and thus be receptacles of *barakah.*

An essential trait distinguishing man from animals is that man knows he must die, whereas animals do not. Now this knowledge of death is a proof of immortality; it is only because man is immortal that his faculties enable him to take cognizance of his earthly impermanence. To say consciousness of death is to say religious phenomenon; and let us specify that this phenomenon is a part of ecology in the total sense of the term; for without religion — or without authentic religion — a human collectivity cannot survive in the long run; that is, it cannot remain human.

\*

\* \*

The human being, when defined or described according to the principle of duality, is divided into an outward man and an inward man; one being sensorial-cerebral and terrestrial, and the other intellective-cardiac and celestial. When defined according to the principle of trinity, he is divided into intelligence, will and sentiment; according to the principle of quaternity, he will be composed of reason, intuition, memory and imagination; these constitute so to speak two axes, one "vertical" and the other "horizontal."

Now it is the principle of trinity that takes precedence, in the sense that it is the happy medium between synthesis and analysis: it is more explicit than duality and more essential than quaternity; being closer to unity than the even numbers, trinity reflects more directly Being itself.

*
* *

Supreme Reality equals Sovereign Good.

Being absolute, the Supreme Reality is infinite; the same is true of the Sovereign Good, which is absolute Reality conceived of in terms of its nature or its content.

In the world, every reality as such bears witness to the Supreme Reality, to Reality in Itself. And similarly, every good as such bears witness to the Sovereign Good, to the Good in Itself.

Human intelligence, or the intellect, cannot disclose to us the aseity of the Absolute, and no sensible person would ask this of it; the intellect can give us points of reference, and this is all that is necessary as regards discriminative and introductory knowledge, the knowledge that can be expressed through words. But the intellect is not only discriminative, it is also contemplative, hence unitive, and in this respect it cannot be said to be limited, any more than a mirror limits the light which is reflected in it; the contemplative dimension of the intellect coincides with the ineffable.[7]

---

7. A pernicious error that must be pointed out here — one which seems to be axiomatic with the false gurus of East and West — is what could be designated by the term "realizationism": it is claimed that only

It is often argued, in a theological climate, that the human intellect is too weak to know God; now the reason for being of the intellect is precisely this knowledge, indirect and indicative in a certain respect, and direct and unitive in another. An incontrovertible proof of God is that the human spirit is capable of objectivity and transcendence, transcendence being the sufficient reason of objectivity. This is not to say that such a proof is necessary to knowledge, but that it is in the nature of things and that it corroborates ab extra what the intellect perceives ab intra, given that metaphysical certitude has its roots in what we are.

*

*   *

Each of the prerogatives of the human state, being in its own way a cosmos, comprises two poles, an active and a passive, or a dynamic and a static. Thus for the intelligence there are discernment and contemplation, analysis and synthesis, or again, in a more subjective and empirical sense, certitude and serenity; in the will, there is the distinction between decision and perseverance, initiative and stability; and in the soul, or sentiment, between fervor and faithfulness.

Certitude and serenity, or faith and peace: peace emanates from faith, just as the Infinite — or All-Possibility — prolongs in a way the Absolute. To live, man needs peace; now, it is vain to seek this peace outside metaphysical and eschatological certitudes, to which our spirit is proportioned

"realization" counts and that "theory" is nothing, as if man were not a thinking being, and as if he could undertake anything whatsoever without knowing where he was going. False masters speak readily of "developing latent energies"; now one can go to hell with all the developments and all the energies one pleases; it is in any case better to die with a good theory than with a false "realization." What the pseudo-spiritualists lose sight of only too easily is that, according to the maxim of the maharajahs of Benares, "there is no right superior to that of the truth."

because it is human and which it must assimilate because, precisely, it is proportioned to them. One would like to say with Saint Bernard, but in paraphrasing him: *"O beata certitudo, o certa beatitudo!*[8]

\*

\* \*

To recapitulate: the prerogatives of the human state consist essentially of intelligence, will and sentiment, capable of objectivity and transcendence. Objectivity is the "horizontal" dimension: it is the capacity to know, to will and to love things as they are, thus without any subjectivistic deformation; while transcendence is the "vertical" dimension: it is the capacity to know, to will and to love God and, ipso facto, all the precious things that lie beyond our earthly experience and which relate more or less directly to the Divine Order.

But by no means are these capacities actualized in every human being. To begin with, too many men have no metaphysical knowledge; then, too many men, if they do have it, do not know how to make it enter into their will and their love, and this cleavage between thought and the individual soul is something much more serious, even, than lack of knowledge. In fact, if metaphysical knowledge remains purely mental, it is worth practically nothing; knowledge is of value only on condition that it be prolonged in both love and will. Consequently, the goal of the Way is first of all to mend this hereditary break, and then — on that foundation — to bring about an ascension towards the Sovereign Good, which, in virtue of the mystery of immanence, is our own true Being.

Man is made of objectivity and transcendence; having forgotten this — existentially even more than mentally —

---

8. "Certitude" in place of "solitude." Solitude in God has nothing privative about it, given the Infinitude of the Sovereign Good; man is "alone" because God is "one," but this Unity is Totality.

his quasi-ontological vocation is to "become again what he is," which means, to return to his celestial potentiality. Without objectivity and transcendence there cannot be man, there is only the human animal; to find man, one must aspire to God.

# Man in the Cosmogonic Projection

The creative radiation coincides with the mystery of existential *Māyā* — that is, not with *Māyā* as such, which at its summit includes the existentiating Principle. The entire world is *Māyā*, but *Māyā* is not entirely the world. The divine Essence, "Beyond Being," reverberates in Relativity, giving rise to the Divine Person, to Creative "Being."[1]

The question of the "why" of creation has given rise to many speculations. We have more than once answered them during the course of our expositions: the cosmogonic projection has as its ultimate cause the infinitude proper to the Absolute. Now, to say infinitude is to say All-Possibility and consequently the overflowing of the divine potentialities, in conformity with the principle that the Good wills to communicate itself. It is said that God "created" the world by "a free act of His will," but this is only to stress that God does not act under constraint; this last term somehow lends itself to confusion for it goes without saying that God is indeed "obliged" to be faithful to His Nature and for that reason cannot but manifest Himself by a quasi-eternal or co-eternal chain of creations,[2] a chain that, pertaining to the cosmic

---

1. This is to say that the personal God pertains to *Māyā*, of which He is the center or the summit, otherwise He could not be an interlocutor for man.

2. As is taught notably by the Hindus and the Greeks. Metaphysical necessity is not constraint any more than liberty is arbitrariness.

17

*Māyā*, could not affect the transcendence of even the personal Divinity.

The productions of the creative radiation are both successive and simultaneous: they are successive inasmuch as they construct the world or emerge into its space, and they are simultaneous inasmuch as, the world being now unfolded, they constitute its hierarchic structure. Universal projection does not imply any "emanation" in the literal and conventional sense of the term, and in any case it excludes all transformist evolution, even though superficial adaptations to a given environment are always possible. We refer here to principles which by their nature elude empirical investigations but not pure intellection, intellectual intuition being rooted in the very substance of the human spirit, without which *homo* would not be *sapiens*.

*
* *

At first sight, it might be thought that the end result of the cosmogonic projection is matter, which in fact appears as the "final point" of the existentiating trajectory; but it is so only in a certain respect, that of the cosmic Substance, of which it is the most exteriorized and contingent mode; it is such at least for our sensorial world, for one can conceive of indefinitely more "solidified" substances than the matter pertaining to our spatial cosmos.[3]

From an altogether different standpoint, we would say that the end result of the manifesting trajectory is not a given substance-container but the form-content, namely the thing created, the more or less distant reflection of a given divine archetype. The reflections of the "ideas" embrace not only positive phenomena but also negative phenomena, inas-

---

3. For the evolutionists, this matter is the very theater — or the initial substance — of universal Possibility; gratuitous concepts such as those of the biosphere or of the "noosphere" add nothing that could attenuate this error whose effects are incalculable.

much as these comprise positive elements on pain of not being able to exist; a bad creature possesses at least, and necessarily, the gift of existence and in addition given qualities or given faculties. In the respect at issue, cosmic manifestation is basically a good because it represents the qualities of Being.

Another mode of cosmic projection is what we could term the "privative accident": this projection directly expresses the movement away from the divine Source. Manifestation is not the Principle, the effect is not the cause; that which is "other than God" could not possess the perfections of God, hence in the final analysis and within the general imperfection of the created, there results that privative and subversive phenomenon which we call evil. This is to say that the cosmogonic ray, by plunging as it were into "nothingness," ends by manifesting "the possibility of the impossible"; the "absurd" cannot but be produced somewhere in the economy of the divine Possibility, otherwise the Infinite would not be the Infinite. But strictly speaking, evil or the devil cannot oppose the Divinity, who has no opposite; it opposes man who is the mirror of God and the movement towards the divine.

A mode that compensates and in a certain sense overcomes the phenomenon of evil, and which even crowns all the other modes, is "reintegration": the cosmogonic movement is not merely centrifugal, it becomes centripetal in the final analysis, which is to say that it is circular; the circle of *Māyā* closes in the heart of deified man. In this respect the end result of the cosmogonic projection is man, or more specifically, the intellect perceiving the Absolute, and then the will drawing the consequences from this perception. To the question of knowing why man has been placed in the world when his fundamental vocation is to leave it, we would reply: it is precisely in order that there be someone who returns to God; this is to say that All-Possibility requires that God not only project Himself, but also realize the liberating beatitude of the return. Just as a mirror realizes in its way

19

the sun that is reflected therein, so man realizes his divine Model; firstly by his theomorphic nature and then by the consequences that it implies. In addition to this mode of cosmic projection that is the human phenomenon there is a so to speak secondary but intrinsically central mode, namely the avataric mode, the "divine Descent," the Incarnation; supreme mode of the projection of *Ātmā-Māyā*. In the framework of fallen humanity, and owing to this fall, the initial human projection is repeated by the *Avatāra* in order to reestablish equilibrium and to restore to man his first vocation; it is to this that the symbolism of the dance of the *gopis* around Krishna testifies.

*

\* \*

Animality can manifest modes of fall as well as modes of perfection, but the animal species cannot fall; only man, participating in the divine liberty and created in order to freely choose God, can make a bad use of his freedom under the influence of that cosmic mode that is evil. Whatever the case — if we may use a somewhat unexpected symbolism — just as the boomerang by its very form is destined to return to him who has thrown it, so man is predestined by his form to return to his divine Prototype; whether he wills it or not, man is "condemned" to transcendence.

Humanly speaking, the privative and subversive cosmic ray is none other than the *princeps hujus mundi;* the worst of perversions is that of man because *corruptio optimi pessima.* The "dark" and "descending" tendency not only moves away from the Sovereign Good, but also rises up against It; whence the equation between the devil and pride. And this permits us to insert here the following consideration: altogether close to pride are doubt, bitterness and despair; the great evil for man is not only to move away from God, it is also to doubt in His Mercy. It is to overlook that at the very depths of the abyss the lifeline is always there: the Divine Hand is held out, provided we have the humility and the faith that allow us to grasp it. The cosmic projection moves away from God, but this movement can have nothing absolute about it; the Center is present everywhere.

It is in the nature of evil to insinuate itself in all orders to the extent possible: to be sure, every creature has the right to live in the ambience that nature has assigned to it, but in man this right gives rise to the vices of outwardness, superficiality, worldliness, in short, to naive and irresponsible horizontality. Yet the pitfall is not only in the tempting ambience, it is already in the human condition as such, namely in the abuse of intelligence: this can be characterized by the terms titanism, icarism, babelism, scientism and civilizationism. Moreover, there is no excess that does not have its indirect source in some truth or reality; thus nihilism and despair could refer, although abusively, to the universal illusion; or let us say to the aspect of illusion of the cosmogonic projection. In an inversely analogous manner, the aspect of identity that reduces or leads *Māyā* back to *Ātmā* gives rise indirectly and caricaturally to the self-worship of certain pseudo-vedantists, and also to idolatry in general; the image is taken for the real thing, the empirical "I" for the immanent Self, the psychic for the spiritual; *quod absit*.

*

\*   \*

Man, we have said, has been placed in the world so that there be in it someone who may return to God. This is what is suggested, among other signs, by that "supernaturally natural" theophany that is the human body: man being *imago Dei*, his body necessarily symbolizes a liberating return to the divine origin and in this sense it is "remembrance of God." It is true that the noble animal — such as the stag, the lion, the eagle, the swan — also expresses a given aspect of the divine Majesty, but it does not manifest the liberating return of the form to the Essence; it remains in the form, whence its "horizontality." The human body on the contrary is "vertical"; it is a sacrament, whether it be masculine or feminine; the difference of the sexes marks a complementarity of mode and not, quite clearly, a divergence of principle. Sacred nudity — in India for example — expresses the exteriorization of that which is most interior and correlatively the interiorization of that which is most exterior; "and that is why, naked, I dance," as Lalla Yogishwari said after having realized the immanent Self. Extremes meet; the natural form can be the vehicle of the supernatural essence, and the latter can be manifested by the former.

Mentalities having little familiarity with the proceedings of symbolism might contest the physical deiformity of man by arguing, for example, that God has neither a frontal nor a posterior side and that He could not walk since He is immutable. This is obvious when one takes things literally, but it is important to understand that the incommensurable levels of the points of comparison do not abolish analogy nor consequently symbolism.[4] The posterior side which may be considered here, is none other than *Māyā* inasmuch as it separates Being from non-Being; the frontal side is Being inasmuch as It conceives the possibilities to be projected into the space of *Māyā;* and God's walk is that very projection. Being, since it pertains to *Māyā,* turns its back on Beyond-Being while remaining united with it in respect of the Essence; and it turns its face towards *Māyā* by the very fact that it existentiates the potentialities that will make up the world. Finally we would say that the Creator's progression is noble: it possesses the quality of beauty in the sense that in manifesting the archetypes God always observes the hierarchy of things; but it goes without saying that the Supreme Principle cannot go out of Itself. The "divine walk" in and by *Māyā* is, so to speak, a "dream" of the Divinity, Who always

---

4. Keeping to what relates to our deiformity, we would point out — strange as it may seem — that anatomy is independent of biological rigors and impurities, which pertain to the cosmic level and not to the archetype; they are perversions due to our fall into post-paradisaical matter, and privatively reflect archetypal hence heavenly functions.

remains unique and immutable; it is only for the creatures that this dream is an exteriorization, a *creatio ex nihilo* precisely.[5]

There is no virtue that does not derive from God, and there is none that He does not possess; this allows raising the question of knowing whether He possesses the virtue of humility, which by definition pertains to the creature; a question that is paradoxical and ill-sounding, to say the least, but logically inevitable. The answer is that the personal God, quite clearly, is in no way opposed to the suprapersonal Divinity of which He existentiates certain potentialities; Being could not contradict Beyond-Being. The God-Person is so to speak "subject" to his own Essence, the "pure Absolute";[6] the divine Unity — or the homogeneity of the Divine Order — is not impaired by the degrees of reality. To say that God is "one" does not mean that principial Reality does not comprise degrees, but that Being is unique and indivisible; it nonetheless possesses qualities and faculties, lacking which creatures would not possess them. But let us return to the question of humility: just as the personal God is "subject," hence in a certain sense "humble," in relation to the Suprapersonal Divinity, so too man ought to show himself humble in relation to his own heart-intellect, the immanent divine spark; the proud man sins against his own immortal essence as well as against God and men.

With all these considerations — no doubt little known but all the more instructive in some respects — we intend to show that universal correspondences are not limited to

---

5. *Brahman satyam, jagan mithyam:* "*Brahman* is reality, the world is appearance." Let it be noted that the vedantists do not insist in an exclusive manner on the negative aspect of illusion; it is important in fact to combine the idea of unreality with that of relative reality. "Mirage" is not a synonym for "nothingness"; the apparently absurd notion of a "relative nothingness" is as inescapable as that of a "relatively absolute."

6. This expression is not a tautology since we have in view the presence of *Māyā* in the Divine Order.

fundamental images but also include the secondary aspects of the key-symbols.[7] In any case, and despite all the evident analogies between the celestial and terrestrial orders, it must be clearly understood that in respect of incommensurability there is nothing in the world that resembles God.

*
*  *

When it is affirmed that "God is beyond the opposition between good and evil"[8] this does not mean that for God evil does not exist as such, but that God sees things in all the relationships involving them and that consequently evil for God is only a fragmentary, provisional, and altogether extrinsic aspect of a good which compensates and ultimately annuls it. In other words, God perceives evil only in its metaphysically indispensable context: in connection, on the one hand, with the good that the evil contradicts and thereby throws into relief, and on the other hand with the good which will overcome it because *vincit omnia Veritas.*

It has been said, in Sufic surroundings, that God has no need to love and that moreover He has no need of our love; this is ill-sounding owing to the ambiguity of the term "God," which a priori applies to the personified Divinity, while in the above-mentioned opinion what is in question is quite obviously the suprapersonal Divinity, which precisely is not an interlocutor for man. That Beyond-Being is the essence of love makes no difference, given that absolute Reality has no object of love outside Itself; in other words,

---

7. The Platonic ideas have been blamed for accounting only for certain phenomena and for excluding others and above all for excluding the contingent aspects of things; an unjust reproach, for every phenomenal possibility, as regards what is essential in it, allows itself to be connected to an archetypal root lacking which there would be phenomena independent of any principle.

8. Such formulations are found above all in Moslem authors, always concerned with safeguarding at any price the unity of the divine Will, which theological anthropomorphism sometimes makes difficult.

the bipolarity subject-object is transcended in Beatitude. Let us specify that for Beyond-Being we do not exist; it is only "as Being" that the Absolute conceives our existence.[9]

We have said that God perceives evil only in its indispensable metaphysical context; this "divine perspective" — if such an expression be permissible — must be repeated in the human soul, and is even the first condition for the "way of return" we have spoken of before. Far from enclosing himself in a "horizontal" perspective that considers things in isolation and as if they were absolute, "ascending" man never loses sight of that "categorically imperative" point of reference that is God: he sees things in their divine context, not by an accidental effort but by a profound disposition of the heart. From this viewpoint derive all the qualities that give meaning to life: humility and charity, that is to say self-knowledge and compassion towards others; resignation to the will of Heaven and trust in Mercy, or fear and love. Or again: discernment of the absolutely Real logically entails discernment of the relatively real, namely also of the ego, whence the virtue of humility; similarly, union with the divine Self entails union with our neighbor and this is the virtue of charity.[10] It is thus that humility and charity, rightly understood and applied, are the criteria of sincerity for metaphysical discernment on the one hand and mystical union on the other.

\*
\* \*

9. The great pitfall of the monotheistic theologies is the de facto confusion between the two levels. There is no "God" which in one and the same respect is Being and Beyond-Being, Person and Essence, *Gott* and *Gottheit, Ishvara* and *Paramātmā;* a personal will is one thing, All-Possibility is another.

10. "Inasmuch as ye have done it unto one of the least of these my brethren, ye have done it unto Me." The divine Self is subjectively immanent in ourselves and objectively immanent in others; objectively from our point of view, but subjectively from theirs, for they are "I" just as we are.

Man's spiritual alchemy comprises two dimensions, or two phases, which can be designated by the terms "doctrine" and "method," or "truth" and "way." The first element appears as the divine Word, and the second as the human response; in this sense the truth is a descent, and the way an ascent.

That being said, let us return to our starting point. *Ātmā* became *Māyā* so that *Māyā* might become *Ātmā;*[11] the reason for this is that the divine All-Possibility, which coincides with Infinitude, implies the possibility for God to be known "from without" and starting from an "other than He"; there lies the whole meaning of the creation of man and even of creation as such. At the level of Being, the Sovereign Good becomes differentiated and the resulting qualities become exteriorized; without an Absolute making itself relativity there would be no world.

To be sure, the cosmogonic projection draws away from God, but this is in the sense of a *felix culpa;* the Bible attests to this: "And God saw that it was good." In Buddhist language: "May all beings be happy"; this is to say that beyond the cycles of existence the last word belongs to Beatitude, which coincides with Being, and thereby with the essence of all that is.

11. We paraphrase here in Vedantic terms the famous formula of St. Ireneus, which enunciates the reciprocity between God and man and thereby the cosmogonic circuit. For the human microcosm the result of this circuit is Paradise; for the macrocosm, "universal Man" *(al-Insān al-Kāmil)* of the Sufis, the end result is the apocatastasis.

# The Play of Masks

When humanity is considered from the standpoint of its values, it is necessary to distinguish a priori between the man-center, who is determined by the intellect and is therefore rooted in the Immutable, and the man-periphery, who is more or less an accident. This difference is repeated — mutatis mutandis — in every man who is conscious of the supernatural, whether he belongs to the first category or the second; without this awareness he has no authentic centrality nor consequently any decisive worth. That is the meaning of the Eckhartian distinction between the "inner man" and the "outer man": the latter identifies passively with his experiences, whereas the former may enjoy or suffer in his temporal humanity, while remaining impassible in his immortal kernel which coincides with his state of union with God. The possibility of such a parallelism lies in man's very nature, and is the essence of the notion of the *avatāra;* in this respect — analogically speaking and with all due proportion — every pneumatic is "true man and true God." The underlying divine substance does not abolish the human mask, any more than the mask prevents the divine manifestation.[1]

---

1. The play of Krishna with the *Gopis* refers to the masks; the apparition of his immutable form before Arjuna refers to the divine Substance. This form, reflected in *Māyā,* assumed in its turn innumerable masks, not earthly but celestial.

It has been said that there are saintly men who "laugh with those who laugh and weep with those who weep"; which indirectly expresses the detachment, and directly the good will, of the "pneumatic" or "central" man. He is detached because he does not identify with the accidents; and he is good-willed because, for that very reason, he could be neither egoistic nor petty; but his very superiority poses for him problems of adaptation, for on the one hand he must form part of the human ambience, and on the other he cannot grasp immediately all its absurdity.[2] The man-center is necessarily situated in an isolation from which he cannot but suffer "externally": feeling that every man is in a certain way like himself, he sincerely puts himself in their place, but it is far from the case that others put themselves in his. Moreover, the ways of acting of the man-center may be "amoral," although not "immoral": they may be contrary to a particular morality, but not to morality as such; thus it is proper to discern between a "justice" that is extrinsic and conditional and another that is intrinsic and unconditional.

On the other hand and in a general way, it is obviously necessary to distinguish between the mask out of charity and the mask of malice; the latter is insincere, the former is sincere. In ordinary language, the word "mask" is synonymous with "false appearance," hence with insincerity; this is plausible from the standpoint of ordinary psychology, but it is to lose sight of the fact that there are sacred masks and

2. In *Hamlet,* Shakespeare puts forth the image of a contemplative but dreamy and passional man: in the first respect, the hero remains a stranger to the absurdity of the world; in the second, he himself becomes enmeshed in this incoherence. It should be noted that the work of a playwright of necessity refers to the cosmic phenomenon of the innumerable masks that differentiate the human person; natural masks that are unaware of being masks, precisely, whereas an actor is aware of it and thus can "realize" the profound meaning of his protean art. The emperor Augustus, who was divinized while still living, is supposed to have said before dying: "Applaud, for have I not played well the comedy of life?" This indicates in its way the distance of the "pneumatic" in relation to the "psychic" and the "hylic."

priestly vestments which express either what transcends the wearer, or on the contrary express his transcendent substance itself. It is thus, moreover, that in historical religions an *upāya* serves as the vestment of the "naked truth," the primordial, perennial and universal religion: symbolism transmits the heavenly Message and at the same time dissimulates the provisionally unassimilable mystery.

There is a difference in function, in principle at least, between the veil and the mask: the latter is positive in the sense that it expresses, affirms, manifests, whereas the former is negative because it dissimulates and thus renders inaccessible. We could also say that, by the veil one wishes to appear "less than one is" since one desires to "vanish"; by the mask on the contrary, one wishes to appear to be "more than one is," since one's intention is to express something that one is not, unless the mask serves to manifest the very "heart" of the wearer and to specify thereby a personal value — which actually is transpersonal — and which otherwise would remain invisible. However, there are cases wherein wisdom takes on the appearance of naivety — or even absurdity — whether involuntarily through lack of experience in an inferior environment,[3] or voluntarily in virtue of a vocation of hiding wisdom, and thereby of ostentatious paradox;[4] this possibility is one that cannot be excluded from the gamut of human attitudes, nor with all the more reason from divine All-Possibility.

---

3. However: "Whoso can do the greater, can do the lesser"; this is obvious, but it presupposes that the ambience be intelligible to the superior man situated in it, for he may not understand the psychological functioning of a given sin or vice; he comes from "another planet," and moreover bears it within himself.

4. The names of Diogenes and Omar Khayyam, and perhaps even those of Nasruddin Khoja and Till Eulenspiegel, could be cited here. The court fools pertain in principle to the same rather ambiguous category as do the *heyoka* of the Red Indians, not to mention the "fools of God" who can be encountered in various religious environments.

\*

\*    \*

We mentioned above the isolation of the man-center in the face of the world's absurdity; now the fact that his behavior can be like that of the man-periphery may give the impression of solidarity with the worldly ambience, but this is a deceptive appearance, since similar ways of acting can hide dissimilar intentions. Aside from the fact that the superior man may behave "like others" to mask his superiority, precisely — either out of charity or out of an "instinct" for self-preservation — there is this to consider, and it is essential: for the contemplative man, pleasure does not inflate the individuality; on the contrary, it invites to a transpersonal dilation, so that the "sensible consolation" gives rise to an upward opening and not to a downward inflation.[5] Moreover, an analogous grace intervenes for every sincere believer when he approaches pleasure "in the name of God" and thus opens himself to Mercy: he "invites" God and at the same time takes refuge in Him.

Extrinsically — in relation to human weakness — the moral norm may be "counter to nature"; intrinsically, it is not so. "They have no wine," said Mary at the wedding at Cana, with an intention that could not be limited to the "flesh," any more than the symbolisms of the Song of Songs or of the Gita Govinda. Ascesis is useful or necessary for

5. The in principle equivocal character of pleasure appears in a particularly flagrant manner in music, which inebriates in two opposite directions, self-love and the sense of the Infinite; it can invite to narcissism as well as to contemplative self-transcending. Meister Eckhart wrote somewhere that every meal has a sacramental import for souls deeply united to God; thus pleasure, to the extent of its effectiveness, excludes the mechanism of passional falling away, whether the person involved be a hermit or polygamous. "Water takes on the color of its receptacle," said Al-Junayd, which implies that pleasure takes on the nature of the man enjoying it; in other words, the nature of the subject determines the relationship between the subject and the object.

man such as he is in fact — for man excluded from the earthly and heavenly Paradises — but the ascetical perspective could not for that reason be endowed with the whole truth, nor consequently with legitimacy pure and simple. The partisans of a touchy asceticism readily overlook the fact that men are not all alike: no doubt, every amusement is a pleasure, but it does not follow that every pleasure is an amusement, otherwise every marriage would be something frivolous, including the wedding at Cana.

Not only truth, merit and sacrifice lead to God, but also beauty; creation itself testifies to this, then sacred art, including liturgy, the forms of worship. Not only error, crime and lust remove from God, but also ugliness; not when it is accidental, for then it is neutral,[6] but when it is willed and produced, as is the case of that universe of organized and desperate ugliness which is the modern world. Besides, vice is a kind of ugliness, as virtue is a kind of beauty; "thou art all fair, my love, there is no spot in thee."

Man's deformity implies moral beauty, if only — de facto — as a potentiality. The pneumatic is a man who identifies a priori with his spiritual substance and thus always remains faithful to himself; he is not a mask unaware of his scope, as is the man enclosed in accidentality.

\*

\* \*

*Jīvātmā*, the "living soul," is the mask-individual that is illusorily and innumerably superimposed on *Ātmā*, or on the one "Self." Now the individual as such identifies with contingency, and for that reason is subject to the principles of limitation and fluctuation; limitation, because no formal perfection can include all other perfections, and fluctua-

---

6. And neutralized by a context of beauty; herein lies, in a certain sense, the meaning of the gargoyles on cathedrals. However, one does not blame a man for being ugly, but one may blame him for the ugliness of his expression.

tion, because temporal manifestation is subject to phases or to alternations — namely, to activity and passivity — and although this takes away nothing from perfection as such, it can nonetheless disfigure it. The phase of activity favors man's natural freedom; but the phase of passivity renders man more vulnerable in relation to his ambience and thus to his own weaknesses, whether they be substantial or accidental. In a word, contingency is made of inequality, in time as in space, without this necessarily implying — it must be insisted upon — intrinsic imperfections.[7] Let us specify that there is not only the temporal fluctuation between the active and passive phases, but also the as it were spatial disequilibrium between man's outward and inward dimensions. The ideal is, on the one hand, the victory of spiritual activity over the passive phase, and on the other, the victory of spiritual inwardness over the outward dimension.

The problem of equilibrium is particularly related to the pull between the exteriorizing or manifesting function and the interiorizing or reintegrating function: there are sages whose sole duty is to attract souls towards the "within," and this is the rule; there are others who add to this function that of creating sensible supports, and this is the exception; the most obvious and evident example of this is the "culture hero" *(Kulturheros)* who inaugurates a civilization or a period of culture.[8] And the following distinction is essential: there is an exteriorization that is profane and amounts to a choice of the "world" as against the spirit; there is another that is spiritual, whose end is interiorization, the way towards the

7. It is this that explains the states of "aridity" or "dryness" from which mystics may suffer; in these states they are particularly exposed to temptations or to inner trials.

8. By painting the first icon of the Blessed Virgin, St. Luke introduced painting into Christianity and created the entire artistic dimension of this religion, which has been maintained in the Eastern Church. In an analogous manner, Jalal ad-Din Rumi introduced music and dance into Sufism, not out of invention, of course, but through inspiration.

"kingdom of God"; for every man endowed with a minimum degree of spirituality, the criterion of the balance between the outward and the inward is the predominance of the internal pole of attraction. The "man of prayer" is capable of measuring what he is able to offer to his ambience, and what he is able to accept from it, without dispersing himself and without being unfaithful to his vocation of inwardness; nothing should be to the detriment of our relationship with immanent Heaven. Only those who give themselves to God can know what they have a right, or duty, to give to the world and to receive from it.

Aside from limitation, fluctuation and disequilibrium, there is impermanence, which is temporal limitation; in one and the same life, childhood, youth, maturity pass, as does life itself.[9] Normally, youth and maturity constitute the manifestation of the prototype or the "idea," for childhood and old-age have something privative in them: the child is "not yet," and the old man is "no longer." However, the summit of individual manifestation is not always situated in youth or in maturity: certain individuals manifest their best possibility in childhood after which they harden or become heavy; others manifest it only in old age. Of course, a peak manifestation at maturity need not preclude the same from occurring in old age: an *avatāra*, who is of necessity a perfect man in every respect, will necessarily manifest the perfection of each age; this is also possible for men of a less lofty category, and even for men who are modestly endowed but nonetheless marked by a heavenly favor.

\*
\* \*

9. "All that appears deserves to disappear" *(Denn alles, was entsteht, ist wert, dass es zugrunde geht)*, said Goethe in his *Faust*, wherein he confuses in a way God's destructive function with the corrosive function of the devil; the saying nonetheless expresses a certain "logic" inherent in creaturely *māyā*.

"The just sin seven times daily": this contradiction in terms has the function of making it understood that in this lower world perfection cannot be absolute, except in the sense of "relative absoluteness"; without this reservation, one would be able to do without the notion of perfection. According to Moslem esoterism, "no sin compares with that of existence"; thus the Sufi asks forgiveness of God morning and night, possibly without being aware of any evil;[10] he accuses himself because he exists. "Why callest thou me good?" said Christ; "there is none good but one, that is, God"; which obviously could not mean that there is the least blemish in deified man.

If on the one hand man is subject to limitations, dimensions, phases — owing in large measure to his connection with matter — on the other hand he can be either fundamentally good or fundamentally bad, depending on his individual substance which pertains to the play of All-Possibility; it is the possibilities that "want" to be what they are, it is not God who imposes it upon them. And this is unrelated to the general modes of contingency such as space and time; the direct cause of personal character resides not in matter nor in other external factors, but in the spirit, in the individual sense of this term. The good manifests qualities, the bad on the contrary manifests privations; but both alike are subject to the vicissitudes of existence.

The combination of fundamental characters and the modes of earthly contingency gives rise to an indefinite diversity of types and destinies;[11] thus the relativists will

10. If David considered that "mine iniquities . . . are more than the hairs of mine head," it is because, as a Semitic fideist and moralist — not a "philosopher" as the Aryan Greeks and Hindus — he "subjectivizes" his objective awareness of the dissonances of relativity.

11. "Whoso willeth, cannot; whoso can, willeth not; whoso knoweth, doeth not; whoso doeth, knoweth not; and thus it goeth ill with the world." *(Chi vuo, non puo; chi puo, non vuo; chi sa, non fa; chi fa, non sa; e così il mondo mal va.)* This Italian saying, with its proverbial quality, in its way sums up well the misery of the "human comedy," and ipso facto that of earthly contingency.

conclude that nothing is good or evil in itself, there is only "more" or "less"; which is flagrant nonsense. It is to overlook a distinction — apparently absurd but metaphysically essential — which we have mentioned above, namely that between the "pure absolute" and the "relatively absolute"; the first is the good as such, and the second, the good through participation, or the good "projected into the stuff of evil," if one may express it thus.[12]

We have said above that the limitations, dimensions and phases that govern man may result from his connection with matter; in fact, they govern only the physical and the psychic and not intelligence as such; *corpus* and *anima* and not *spiritus*. The body and the soul are two masks superimposed on the spirit, which in its substance remains unlimited and immutable; and this takes us back to the Eckhartian concept of the "inner man."

Perhaps we should add here a consideration that, although not pertaining directly to our subject, is nonetheless connected with it. According to a Hindu expression, "The Lord is the only transmigrant," which means He goes from birth to birth crossing the chain of the worlds. This is true in the sense of *līlā*, the "divine play," but not if one concludes that individuals are not real at their own level and that they are not responsible for their actions.[13]

\*

\* \*

12. The notion "relatively absolute" could not imply that there is an "absolutely relative," for this expression — aside from its intrinsic absurdity — is practically synonymous with "nothingness."

13. It should not be overlooked that it is as a consequence of their actions that they transmigrate, and that the immanent transmigration of the Lord pertains to the onto-cosmological dimension and not to that of concordant actions and reactions. Cf. the chapter "Universal Eschatology" in our book *Survey of Metaphysics and Esoterism*.

Our profound identity is our relationship with God; our mask is the form that we must assume in the world of forms, of space, of time. Our ambience, as well as our personality, necessarily pertain to the particular, not to the Universal; to possible being, not to necessary Being; to relative good, not to the Sovereign Good. Thus there is no need to be disturbed because one lives in one given ambience and not in another; and further, there is no need to be disturbed because one is a given individual rather than some other. Being a person — on pain of inexistence — one must needs be a particular person; that is, "such and such a person" and not the "person as such"; the latter is situated only in the world of the divine ideas, while the former is its reflection within contingency.

What matters is to maintain, starting from possible being, the contact with necessary Being; with the Sovereign Good which is the essence of our relative values, and whose merciful nature includes the desire to save us from ourselves; to deliver us by having us participate in its mystery both living and immutable.

# Ex Nihilo, In Deo

In the expression *creatio ex nihilo*, the word *nihil* determines the meaning of the word *ex:* thus *ex* does not presuppose a substance or a container as is normally the case, it simply indicates the possibility in principle — which possibility is denied precisely by the word *nihil* in regard to creation — rather as the word "with" indicates a possible object even in the expression "with nothing," which in fact means "without object." Hence there is no point in blaming the theological formula in question for suggesting an extra-divine substance and thereby a fundamental dualism;[1] that would amount to playing with words and taking too seriously the small fatalities of language.

Obviously, creation "comes from" — that is the meaning of the word *ex* — an origin; not from a cosmic, hence "created" substance, but from a reality pertaining to the Creator, and in this sense — and in this sense only — it can be said that creation is situated in God. It is situated in Him in respect of ontological immanence: everything in fact "contains" — on pain of being non-existent — on the one hand Being, and on the other a given Archetype or "Idea"; the divine "content" is ipso facto also the "container," and even is so a priori, since God is Reality as such. But things are "outside God" — all sacred Scriptures attest to this —

1. God fashioned Adam "of earth": but earth was created *ex nihilo*, and with it Adam.

in respect of contingency, hence in respect of the concrete phenomena of the world; the Sovereign Good could not be the content of that privative existence — or of that abyss of contingency — that is evil. The ontological and hence "neutral" structure of evil is "in God," but not so evil as such; in other words, privative and subversive possibilities are not *in Deo* except insofar as they testify to Being and therefore to All-Possibility, and not by their negative contents, which paradoxically signify non-existence or the impossible, hence the absurd.

It may be objected that in situating a dimension of the world outside God we postulate an irreducible dualism; this is in fact what we do, but it is on the plane of universal Relativity — the cosmic *Māyā*[2] — which by definition coincides with duality. The absurdity of "two realities" is precisely the mystery of Relativity; it is the possibility of an "other than God"; to say that there are things which are "outside God," means that they are "in *Māyā.*" To suppress this "outside God" — by maintaining that "everything is in God" in every respect — is to suppress *Māyā*, mystery of Infinitude and of "divine paradox."

With the intention of resolving the problem of evil, some have maintained that evil does not exist for God, and consequently that for Him everything is a good, which is inadmissible and ill-sounding. What ought to be said is that God sees the privative manifestations only in connection with the positive manifestations that compensate for them; thus evil is a provisional factor in view of a greater good, of a "victory of the Truth"; *vincit omnia Veritas.*

At the supreme degree of Reality — *Ātmā* or *Brahman* — *Māyā* neither "is" nor "exists"; the question of dualities, of opposition, of good and evil, consequently could not arise. At the degree of metacosmic *Māyā,* the complementary

2. Not metacosmic or divine *Māyā*, which is the same as pure Being, the personal God, the Creator.

oppositions are affirmed — God is at once Rigor and Gentleness, Justice and Mercy, Power and Beauty — but contingency, and with it, evil, are absent; it is only at the degree of cosmic *Māyā* — this moving fabric of circumstances and antinomies — that the "existential vices" can be produced, at one and the same time "in God" and "outside God": "in God," in the sense that every possibility necessarily pertains to All-Possibility, and "outside God" because the Sovereign Good can only contain the archetypal possibilities, which by definition are positive since they describe the potentialities of pure Being.

\*

\* \*

In what follows, our intention is not to recall needlessly an axiom of which no metaphysician is unaware; our intention is simply to draw attention to two different but complementary delimitations of the "space" *Ātmā-Māyā*, which renders inevitable certain repetitions.

Thus, it is known that there are two "ontological regions," the Absolute and the Relative; the first consists of Beyond-Being, and the second, of both Being and Existence, of the Creator and Creation. But there is also another possible distribution of the same realities; in other words, we may envisage two other "regions," namely the Principial and the Manifested; the first category comprises Beyond-Being and Being — this is the "Divine Order" — and the second, Existence, the Universe, the world. This means that Being does not coincide with the "pure Absolute"; it pertains to the Divine Order inasmuch as it is a direct reflection of the Absolute in the Relative, and consequently it is what may be termed paradoxically the "relatively absolute." If the personal God were the Absolute as such, He could not be an interlocutor for man.

The relationship *Ātmā-Māyā* is indirectly affirmed — at the extremity of the cosmogonic trajectory — by two new "regions," the heavenly and the earthly; we say "indirectly" because the celestial world is *Ātmā* only by analogy, in the sense that it is the reflection of the Principle within Manifestation, and this confers upon it, in relation to the world of imperfection and impermanence, a quasi-divine function. Thus the mythologies readily present the "heavens" as the extreme limit of the Divine Order, and not as an infra-divine category; the angels and the archangels of the Semitic cosmologies thus appear as "gods" — *devas* — who, starting from Perfection, govern the imperfect world.

Only the celestial or angelic Center escapes the fissures and vicissitudes of the cosmic periphery — of the inferior *Māyā* or of the *Samsāra* — without thereby being able to escape the limitations proper to Relativity. This distinction is essential: "limitation" is not synonymous with "imperfection"; the sphere is limited in relation to space, but it is in no way imperfect, quite the contrary, since it is the most perfect form possible. In saying that "God alone is good," Christ meant to specify, not that the angels and the blessed are deprived of goodness, but that only the Principial Order — hence the non-manifested — is situated beyond even the accidental possibility of imperfection.

"Our Father who art in heaven," Christ said, thereby indicating the two poles of the Divine Order, namely the God-Person and the celestial world. "Hallowed be Thy Name," and "Thy Kingdom come": the first enunciation evokes the ascent of *Māyā* towards *Ātmā*, of man towards God; and the second, the descent of *Ātmā* towards *Māyā*, of God towards man; this is also expressed — with a different accentuation — by the patristic formula: "God became man that man might become God." The Essence limited itself by form so that the form might be liberated by the Essence: the reason for being of the finite is, not only the differentiated and innumerable manifestation of the Infinite, but also that perfection, or that happiness, which is the return to It.

\*

\* \*

## Ex Nihilo, In Deo

We have said that each ontological degree presents an aspect of either center or periphery according to whether its context is inferior or superior. But there is more: each degree possesses in itself these two aspects, starting with the "dimensions" of absoluteness and infinitude in Beyond-Being; analogously, Being comprises intrinsic and extrinsic qualities, it is "holy" or "wise" in its essence and "just" or "merciful" towards creation. In Heaven, it is possible to distinguish between the supreme Angel — or the Archangels combined — and the other angels, to which are joined the blessed; beneath Heaven, in the "round of births and deaths," the motionless mover — as Aristotle would say — is none other than man who, being "made in the image of God," is open to the Absolute and to Deliverance. Man ipso facto represents the Immutable and the Limitless, to the extent that the extreme limit of Universal Manifestation makes it possible; he represents them potentially, indirectly and passively in the case of ordinary men, but effectively, directly and actively in the case of deified man, who thus is central not only — as is every man — with regard to the animal world, but also — in a particular and additional manner — with regard to the multitude of ordinary men. The "believers" are like the *gopis* dancing around Krishna and uniting themselves to him; whereas he — the "motionless mover" — plays the saving flute.

To say that deified man plays the part of the motionless mover in relation to a human collectivity, means implicitly that Revelation, Tradition, the divine Symbol, or the sacred in general represent this mover. As an example of the Symbol — or of symbolism — we shall mention the circumambulation of the Kaaba,[3] primordial sanctuary; in this rite, the movement is circular like the revolution of the planets;

---

3. This rite is much more ancient than Islam, since it goes back to Abraham; originally, the participants were naked — like the Indians and in part like the *gopis* — which Islam modified by instituting the semi-nudity of the pilgrims.

another example is the Sun Dance around a tree representing the axis "Heaven-Earth"; there the movement is alternatively centripetal and centrifugal like the phases of respiration, which takes us back to the dance of the *gopis* with its two modes, circumambulation and union, precisely. The universal symbol of the wheel combines both types of participation, which refer, finally, to the two fundamental relationships between *Ātmā* and *Māyā,* the analogical and the unitive: manifestation of diversifying Potentiality and reintegration into the original Synthesis.

# In the Face of Contingency

What makes us happy are the phenomena of beauty and goodness and all the other goods that existence borrows from pure Being; what adds shadows to them is contingency, to which they of necessity pertain since, precisely, they exist. Contingency not only brings about all kinds of limitations, beginning with imperfection and impermanence, but also opposes to positive phenomena negative phenomena, and necessarily so, since All-Possibility is infinite and consequently cannot exclude privative possibilities; these cannot but seem absurd, yet at bottom that is their reason for being.

We are situated in contingency, but we live by the reflections of the Absolute, otherwise we could not exist. We live in and by those agents of contingency which are space, time, form, number, matter, individuality; within this framework, every thing that we love is irreplaceable insofar as it is a celestial message, a ray of the Absolute, but at the same time every thing could be different, including our personality; and this plunges us into a climate of relativity, ambiguity, indefiniteness, and inflicts upon us temptations of incertitude and ingratitude.[1] Wisdom is not only to see the archetype through the form or the heavenly in the earthly, it is

1. Hamlet's drama is that of an a priori superior man who immerses — and encloses — himself in contingency, thereby losing contact with the Absolute; the climate of his "complex" of duty and vengeance is tragically incompatible with that of his love for the angelic Ophelia, a love which

43

also to be resigned to contingency; we must indeed be someone and be someplace, even if we are aware of the possibility of being someone else and of being somewhere else, that is, of experiencing a given element of happiness in another form.

There are here two spiritual attitudes or two fundamental virtues to realize, namely resignation to contingency and assimilation of the celestial message. Assimilation first by gratitude and then by interiorization; for everything lies in discovering that ontologically we bear within ourselves that which we love and which in the final analysis constitutes our reason for being. The indetermination — or the fluctuation — of contingency can neither trouble nor overcome us if we realize within ourselves the meaning of the celestial contents.

\*

\* \*

Just as there is a discernment of principial realities, which devolves upon us because we have an intelligence, so too there is a discernment of formal realities — aesthetic as well as moral — which devolves upon us because we have a soul. This is to say that metaphysical comprehension ought to be accompanied by a sense of beauty at every level; conversely, there is no interiorization of the beautiful without a parallel metaphysical knowledge. "Beauty is the splendor of the true": which implies that truth, hence Reality, is the essence of beauty.

The ontological coincidence between the true and the beautiful brings up the question of knowing "why" something is deemed beautiful. According to the subjectivists, it is because it pleases us — which is absurd — whereas in

would have saved him had he understood that love has precedence over hatred and moreover is not opposed to duty. It will be recalled that according to Aristotle, the goal of tragedy is a *katharsis,* a "purification" through the striking spectacle of miseries due to human absurdity.

reality it pleases an intelligent and normal man because it is beautiful, which however does not answer the question of knowing what beauty consists of concretely. Moreover, one has to know what constitutes not only beauty as such, but also a particular beauty; that is to say that every harmonious and positively expressive thing is beautiful at once in a general respect and in a particular one. In a general way, every beautiful thing communicates to us beauty as such, namely the Harmony — or Beatitude — of the Sovereign Good; at the same time and in a particular way, it transmits this Harmony according to a particular aspect or a particular order of contingency, and that is necessarily so since the effect cannot possess the essentiality or the wholeness of the cause. The human body for example is beautiful — in its perfect and normative form — not only because it expresses the dimension *Ānanda* proper to *Ātmā*, but also, and additionally, because it expresses it either in masculine mode or in feminine mode[2] or according to a particular racial language; or again, obviously, according to a particular individual possibility; or, as regards its specific form: it expresses or manifests the adaptation of an integral subjectivity — integral, hence rooted in the consciousness of the Absolute — to a given contingent ambience, namely the earthly world with its categories, its demands, its possibilities; this adaptation is perfect, which is to say that it is in conformity with the nature of Being, and this conformity constitutes an additional element of beauty. Aside from human beauty, there are of course also animal, vegetable, mineral beauties; and from quite another standpoint, there are visual, auditive, mental and psychic beauties, and others still.

---

2. Woman manifests beauty as such, so much so that there is no beauty superior to hers, when contingency has not separated her from her prototype; thus one may discern in beauty as such features of femininity, of passive perfection, of virginal purity, of maternal generosity; of goodness and love.

Beauty has something pacifying and dilating in it, something consoling and liberating, because it communicates a substance of truth, of evidence and of certitude, and it does so in a concrete and existential mode; thus it is like a mirror of our transpersonal and eternally blissful essence. This being said, it is important not to lose sight of the fact that in the confrontation between contingency and the celestial contents projected into it and of which it is the vehicle, it is not solely a question of beauty properly so called — whether of the aesthetic or the moral order — it is also a question of every other factor, large or small, that can legitimately contribute to our happiness; these contents always refer, in indefinitely diverse ways, to celestial Harmony, into which contingency could not bring any privation, any dissonance, any absurdity; in principle we have the right to this Harmony because it is the norm and because it resides in our very substance. And that is why it could be repeated again and again that man's vocation and duty is to become what he is, precisely by freeing himself, inwardly, of the encroaching shadows of this contingent, imperfect and transitory world.

When one speaks of earthly contingency, it is impossible not to mention matter, which in a certain respect is the vehicle par excellence of this contingency: like *Māyā*, matter is spiritually transparent and it can concretely be the vehicle of the celestial messages, but it can also be the door towards that which is below and it has even subjugated humanity by impurity, sickness, old age and death, so that its domain will always be an exile for man. Nonetheless, one must insist on this, the flowers of Paradise are always within reach; exile is but a dream, because contingency is but a veil.

This mention of matter furnishes us the opportunity to make the following remark concerning materialism: nothing is more contradictory than to deny the spirit, or even simply the psychic element, in favor of matter alone, for it is the spirit that denies, whereas matter remains inert and unconscious. The fact that matter can be thought about proves precisely that materialism contradicts itself at its

46

# WORLD WISDOM BOOKS, INC.

Mailing List
P.O. Box 2682
Bloomington, IN 47402-2682

PLACE
STAMP
HERE

PLEASE PRINT

Book in which this card was found _____

NAME _____

ADDRESS _____

CITY & STATE _____

ZIP OR POSTAL CODE _____

COUNTRY _____
(IF OTHER THAN U.S.A.)

*If you wish to receive a copy
of the latest World Wisdom Books brochure
and to be placed on our mailing list
please send us this card.*

PLEASE PRINT

WORLD WISDOM BOOKS, INC.
Mailing List
P.O. Box 2682
Bloomington, IN 47402-2682

Book in which this card was found
_____

NAME _____

ADDRESS _____

CITY & STATE _____

ZIP OR POSTAL CODE _____ COUNTRY _____
                                  (IF OUTSIDE U.S.A.)

starting point, rather as with Pyrrhonism, for which it is true that there is no truth, or with relativism, for which all is relative except this affirmation. Be that as it may, the subjective could not arise from the objective, and to believe otherwise is to understand nothing of subjectivity; the opposite error also exists, with certain people who conclude from the *Vedānta* that the world is a production of our mind, whereas our mind is capable neither of creating nor of preventing the existence of an object. True, the world is a dream, but this dream is not ours since we are contents of it; the absolute Subject escapes us as much as does the absolute Object, hence as much as their supreme indistinction.

\*

\* \*

Contingency implies essentially two principles, that of relativity and that of absoluteness; the latter corresponds geometrically to radii, and the former to concentric circles, given that one refers to the center and the other to the periphery.[3] The principle of relativity wills that things appear other than what they are in fact; at the interior of this deceptive appearance, and by compensation, the principle of absoluteness wills that things be symbolically adequate, that is, in conformity with their reality. But when the principle of absoluteness predominates, the principle of relativity insinuates itself in the sense that the adequate realities are in some fashion limited and consequently do not coincide at every point with their metacosmic prototypes.

For example, the principle of relativity wills that the sun and the stellar vault seem to turn around the earth, but this deceptive appearance could not prevent an intervention of the principle of absoluteness, namely that the sun have precedence over all the other luminaries by its size, its

3. It is significant that Einstein, the promoter of relativism, found "distasteful" the idea that the universe possesses a center.

luminosity, its heat, and moreover that the appearance of the solar and stellar movements symbolize adequately the cosmic cycles and the activity of the heavenly powers in relation to the passivity of the material and psychic world.[4] And likewise, but conversely: the principle of absoluteness wills that the sun, in conformity with objective reality, be the center of the planets' revolution; this does not prevent the principle of relativity from intervening, and it does so by showing, not that the solar orb is not the center of its system, but that it is merely a grain of dust beside other centers and other systems. The image of the sun as unique center is thus an optical illusion in its turn; God alone is "the Center" without any possible reservations.

If one looks at the universe exclusively with the eyes of relativity, one will see only relative things and the universe will be reduced in the final analysis to an inextricable absurdity. If however one sees it with the eyes of absoluteness — of the participation of things in the Absolute — one will essentially see manifestations of the Supreme Principle and, correlatively, images making explicit the relationships between *Ātmā* and *Māyā*.

For the relativists, there is only *Māyā;* but this is contradictory since *Māyā* exists only through its contents, which prolong *Ātmā;* this is to say that *Ātmā* is conceivable without *Māyā,* whereas *Māyā* is intelligible only through the notion of *Ātmā.* Relativity is a projection of the Absolute, or it is nothing; if it is something, that is because the Absolute by definition is also the Infinite and, ipso facto, universal radiation as well. That is why the principle of absoluteness implies a principle of infinitude by virtue of which it is impossible to measure the existential categories in an exhaustive fashion.

---

4. It is in virtue of this analogy between an optical illusion and cosmological realities that Ptolemaic astronomy comprises an aspect of "exact science."

No doubt the plane of contingency comprises a principle of finitude which wills that everything be limited, and which the sceptics readily lay claim to. But this principle — obviously limited — could not prevent the positive contents of contingency from being related to the principle of infinitude, owing to the fact that they manifest the essences and therefore All-Possibility.

There is in contingency an element of indefiniteness and unintelligibility, we could say of "irrationality," which the scientists wish to oblige to be logical and to give up secrets that, precisely, this element does not possess, or does not possess in an assimilable form. To wish to force things is to expose oneself to becoming the plaything of a "genius of absurdity" inherent in cosmic *Māyā*— power of illusion, and also of seduction, whose absence in the economy of universal Possibility is metaphysically inconceivable, and one of whose signs is the serpent in the terrestrial Paradise.[5]

\*

\* \*

One may object that contingency is the equivalent of relativity and thus encompasses, at its summit, the creative Principle — the "personal God" — and for still stronger reasons the celestial world. To this we reply that the notion of contingency coincides with that of relativity only in the infra-celestial order, which symbolically we may qualify as "terrestrial" and not in the celestial and divine Orders, which from the standpoint of contingency — hence of the "earth" — are related to the Absolute,[6] either indirectly or

5. The tempter pushed man into the descending spiroidal path, that of the indefinite, of the accidental, of contingency without end; one must beware though of understanding this in an exclusively moral sense.

6. This leads us back to the idea — paradoxical but in no way absurd — of the "relatively absolute," which has been at issue more than once in our books.

directly.[7] This does not mean that in Heaven there is no possibility that one could term contingent — otherwise there would be no freedom for the blessed — but this contingency is intrinsically determined, and in a sense stabilized and regulated, by the omnipresence of Grace and by the permanence of the beatific vision; we are here, not beyond *Māyā,* of course, but beyond "Transmigration," beyond *Samsāra.*

However that may be, there is certainly a need to distinguish between contingency and relativity. Contingency is always relative, but relativity is not always contingent; that is relative which is either "more" or "less" in relation to another reality;[8] that is contingent which may or may not be, hence which is merely possible. In contingency, as in relativity, there are degrees: man as such comprises eminently more ontological necessity than a particular man, and yet he is contingent in relation to the Creator, who in a certain sense is the Absolute "projected" into relativity, or relativity "prefigured" in the Absolute; there lies the whole mystery of the initial contact between *Ātmā* and *Māyā.*

\*

\* \*

In geometric symbolism, the radii indicate the celestial archetypes or the "ideas"; and the concentric circles, the orders of contingency. This distinction between the celestial content and contingency imposes upon man — who is related to both — a fundamental and decisive choice: to maintain contact with the celestial or the universal by direct-

---

7. This is to say that Being and Beyond-Being *(Ishwara* and *Paramātmā)* "constitute" Divinity — at least from the standpoint of Being, for Beyond-Being suffices unto Itself — whereas the celestial order "participates" in Divinity in the most direct fashion possible.

8. Thus the Creator — Being — is "more" than creation and creatures, but "less" than the pure Absolute — Beyond-Being — which has no interlocutor.

ing himself towards God, or on the contrary to lose this contact and become immersed in the contingent and finally rise up against God; hence ultimately against himself, since beneath the veil of contingency man is attached ontologically to That which is.

The reason for being of the radiation — necessarily centrifugal — of the celestial possibilities is the manifestation of the Sovereign Good; the meaning of evil being this manifestation when it operates by means of contrast; as Master Eckhart said: "The more he blasphemeth, the more he praiseth God." Direct and analogous manifestation on the one hand, and indirect and contrastive manifestation on the other; both modes being realized in function of the infinitude of the divine Possible.

A word concerning metaphysical certitude, or the infallibility of pure intellection, is perhaps called for here. "I think, therefore I am," said Descartes; aside from the fact that our existence is not proven by thought alone, he should have added: "I am, therefore Being is"; or he could have said in the first place: "I think because I am." In any event, the foundation of metaphysical certitude is the coincidence between truth and our being; a coincidence that no ratiocination could invalidate. Contingent things are proven by factors situated within their order of contingency, whereas things deriving from the Absolute become clear by their participation in the Absolute, hence by a "superabundance of light" — according to Saint Thomas — which amounts to saying that they are proven by themselves. In other words, universal truths draw their evidence not from our contingent thought, but from our transpersonal being, which constitutes the substance of our spirit and guarantees the adequacy of intellection.

\*
\* \*

Contingency on the one hand and presence of the Absolute on the other; these are the two poles of our existence.

The divine presence coincides with our consciousness — or with our intellectual and moral evocation — of the Absolute-Infinite, which by definition is the Sovereign Good, since all possible goods derive from It and testify to It. This presence-consciousness, or this evocation, is set into space and time: spatial, it excludes the world which extends indefinitely around us;[9] temporal, it repeats itself and thereby reduces duration, which corrodes us, to the Eternal Present, which liberates us — this Present being the complement of the Infinite Center.

In principle, this consciousness of God is within every man's reach, precisely because he is man; in fact, it has its exigencies: its formal, ritual and traditional conditions, because man has radically turned away from his human vocation by plunging into the world of contingency and by identifying himself with it, whence the profane ego with its tyranny and its vices. The salutary — but excessive — reaction to this situation is an asceticism that seems to want to destroy the ego as such, contrary to the nature of things or to the intention of the Creator; in reality, what is called for is an equilibrium between our consciousness of the Absolute and the divine Manifestation — made of beauty and goodness — which surrounds us everywhere, and which bids us to the "kingdom of God which is within you."

\*

\* \*

Being comprised within the terrestrial *māyā*, we must maintain the balance between temporal disturbances and eternal values; but it is just as necessary to maintain the balance between the beauties of this world and those of the other: between the terrestrial projections and the celestial

9. The discriminative and contemplative abstraction from the world could not exclude our natural contacts with our ambience, which is not merely Eve, but also Mary. There is parallelism, not incompatibility, between the "remembrance of God" and contingent life.

archetypes. Or between analogy or resemblance, and abstraction or incomparability; analogy referring to immanence, and abstraction to transcendence.

The sense of beauty actualized by the visual or auditive perception of the beautiful, or by the corporeal manifestation, whether static or dynamic, of beauty, is the equivalent of a "remembrance of God" if it is balanced by the "remembrance of God" properly so called, which on the contrary demands the extinction of the perceptible. The sensible perception of the beautiful must be answered by the withdrawal towards the suprasensible source of beauty; the perception of sensible theophany demands unitive interiorization.

For some, only the forgetting of the beautiful — of the "flesh" according to them — brings us closer to God, which is obviously a valid point of view in a certain operative respect; according to others — and this perspective is more profound — sensible beauty also brings us closer to God, and even a priori, on the double condition of a contemplativity that has the presentiment of the archetypes through sensible manifestations, and of an interiorizing spiritual activity that eliminates the sensations in view of the intellective and unitive perception of the Essence.

# Delineations of Original Sin

The idea of original sin situates the cause of the human fall in an action; consequently, this fall consists in committing evil actions, sins precisely. The disadvantage of this idea — which nonetheless is providential and efficacious — is that a man who commits no definite sin may believe himself to be perfect, as if it sufficed to do no evil to deserve Heaven; Christan doctrine wards off this temptation by stressing that every man is a sinner; to doubt it is to add two more sins, those of presumption and heresy. In such a climate, one almost feels obligated, if not to sin, at least to see sins everywhere; it is true that there is a definite number of mortal sins, but the venial sins are innumerable, and they become serious when they are habitual, for then they are vices.

Be that as it may, an obligatory *mea culpa* that has nothing concrete in view, is not a panacea and hardly makes us better; but what is altogether different is to be conscious of the presence in our soul of a tendency to "outwardness" and "horizontality," which constitutes, if not original sin properly so called, at least the hereditary vice that is derived therefrom.

In connection with the idea of sin-as-act, let us note in passing that there are behaviors which are sins objectively without being so subjectively, and that there are others which are sins subjectively without being so objectively: a given saint neglects a religious duty because he is in ecstasy, a given hypocrite accomplishes it because he wishes to be admired. This is said in order to recall that actions are valid according to their intentions; however, it is not enough for the intention to be subjectively good, it must also be so objectively.

But let us return to our subject: to affirm that every man is a "sinner" does not amount to saying that no man is capable of abstaining from evil actions, but it certainly means that all men — with the rarest exceptions — succumb to the temptations of "outwardness" and "horizontality"; where there is no temptation of excess in the direction of either the outward or the horizontal, there is no longer either concupiscence or impiety.[1] Assuredly, every man has the right to a certain solidarity with his ambience, as is proven by our faculties of sensation and action, but this right is limited by our complementary duty of inwardness, without which we would not be men, precisely; this means that that pole of attraction which is the "kingdom of God within you" must in the final analysis prevail over the seductive magic of the world.[2] This is expressed by the supreme Commandment which, while teaching us what we must do, also teaches us what we are.

*
* *

The concept of the sin of omission[3] allows us to grasp more firmly the problem of hereditary sin, that sin which

1. Which evokes the case of the "pneumatics" and above all the mystery of the "Immaculate Conception."

2. According to Shankara, the one "liberated-in-this-life" *(jīvan-mukta)* is not he who stands apart from all that is human, it is he who, when he "laughs with those who laugh and weeps with those who weep," remains the supernaturally unaffected witness of the "cosmic play" *(līlā).*

3. According to the Apostle James, he who knows to do good and does not do it, commits a sin; this is the very definition of sin by omission, but at the same time it goes beyond the framework of a formalistic and exoteric morality.

exists in us before our actions. If the requirement of the supreme Commandment is to "love God with all thy heart, and with all thy soul, and with all thy strength, and with all thy mind," it follows that the contrary attitude is the supreme sin, in varying degree since one has to distinguish between hatred of God and simple indifference; nevertheless, God says in the Apocalypse: "So then because thou art lukewarm . . . I will spue thee out of my mouth." If we wish to give the word "sin" its broadest or deepest meaning, we would say that it expresses above all an attitude of the heart; hence a "being" and not a simple "doing" or "not doing"; in this case, the Biblical myth symbolizes a "substance" and not a simple "accident."

Thus it is that original "sin," for the Hindus, is "nescience" *(avidyā)*: ignorance that *"Brahman* is real, the world is illusory," and that "the soul is not other than *Brahman"*; all actions or attitudes contrary to intrinsic and vocational Law *(Dharma)* result from this blindness of heart.

*
* *

Above we have said "horizontality" and "outwardness." To be "horizontal" is to love only terrestrial life, to the detriment of the ascending and celestial path; to be "exteriorized," is to love only outer things, to the detriment of moral and spiritual values. Or again: horizontality is to sin against transcendence, thus it is to forget God and consequently the meaning of life; and outwardness is to sin against immanence, thus it is to forget our immortal soul and consequently its vocation. In assuming that the orignal sin was an action — whatever the form given to it by a particular mythology — we will say, on the one hand, that this action had as its effect the two kinds of neglect just mentioned, and on the other hand, that this neglect predisposes to the indefinite repetition of the original transgression; every sinful action repeats the drama of the forbidden fruit. Primordial perfection was made of "verticality" and "inwardness," as is attested by those two distinctive characteristics of man which are vertical posture and language, the latter coinciding with reason.

Transcendence is objective inasmuch as it concerns the Divine Order in itself, immanence is subjective inasmuch as it refers to the Divine Presence in us; nonetheless there is also a subjective transcendence, that which within us separates the divine Self from the human "I," and an objective immanence, namely the divine Presence in the world surrounding us. To be really conscious of "God-as-Object" is also to be conscious of His immanence, and to be conscious of "God-as-Subject," is also to be conscious of His transcendence.

Inwardness and verticality, outwardness and horizontality:[4] these are the dimensions that make up man in all his greatness and all his littleness. To say transcendence is to say both metaphysical Truth and saving Divinity; and to say immanence is to say transpersonal Intellect and divine Selfhood. Verticality in the face of "our Father who art in heaven," and inwardness in virtue of the "kingdom of God which is within you"; whence a certitude and a serenity that no stratagem of the powers of darkness can take away from us.

\*

\* \*

Eve and Adam succumbed to the temptation to wish to be more than they could be; the serpent represents the possi-

4. In accordance with the principle of the double meaning of symbols, inwardness and verticality are not solely positive, any more than outwardness and horizontality are solely negative. Inwardness means not only depth but also subjectivism, egoism, hardness of self; verticality means not only ascension but also the fall. Similarly, but inversely, outwardness means not only superficiality and dispersion, but also movement towards a center that liberates; and horizontality means not only lowness but also stability.

bility of this temptation. The builders of the Tower of Babel, as well as the Titans, Prometheus and Icarus, wished to put themselves improperly in God's place; they too suffered the humiliating chastisement of a fall. According to the Bible, the forbidden tree was that of the discernment between "good" and "evil"; now this discernment, or this difference, pertains to the very nature of Being; consequently, its source could not be in the creature; to claim it for oneself is to wish to be equal to the Creator, and that is the very essence of sin; of all sin. Indeed, the sinner decides what is good, counter to the objective nature of things; he willingly deludes himself about things and about himself, whence the fall, which is nothing other than the reaction of reality.

The great ambiguity of the human phenomenon resides in the fact that man is divine without being God: Koranically speaking, man gives all creatures their names, and that is why the angels must prostrate before him; except for the supreme Angel,[5] which indicates that man's divinity, and consequently his authority and automony, are relative, although "relatively absolute." Thus it is that the fall of man as such could not be total, as is proven a priori by the nature and destiny of the patriarch Enoch, father of all "pneumatics," so to speak.

For exoterist ideology, esoterism — "gnosis" — can only originate from darkness since it seems to claim the prerogative of the forbidden tree, the spontaneous and autonomous discernment between "good and evil." But this is to overlook the essential, namely that *aliquid est in anima quod est increatum et increabile . . . et hoc est Intellectus.*[6] The fall was, precisely, the rupture between reason and Intellect, the ego and the Self; one could speculate forever on the modes and

5. Or the Archangels, which amounts to the same thing; it is the Divine Spirit which is mirrored directly at the center or the summit of Universal Manifestation.

6. Meister Eckhart: "There is something in the soul which is uncreated and uncreatable . . . and this is the Intellect."

degrees of this rupture, which on the one hand involves the human species and on the other hand could not be absolute.

# On Intention

The primacy of intention stems from the fact that one and the same action — we are not saying every action — may be good or bad according to the intention, whereas the inverse is not true: an intention is not good or bad according to the action.[1] It is not actions that matter primarily, but rather intentions, as common sense as well as traditional wisdom tell us; however, it goes without saying that this could not mean, as some people imagine, that every imperfect or even bad action can be excused by supposing that the intention was good or even by arguing that every intention is basically good merely because it is subjective and that, according to some people, subjectivity is always right.

To excuse, if only partially, a blameworthy action or production by arguing that the intention was good, is meaningful only in the following cases. First: when the negative result is contrary to what the agent willed; such is the case of a child who starts a fire by lighting a candle. Second: when there are serious reasons for supposing that the badness — or imperfection — of the action or production is due only to

1. Pascal mistakenly attributed to the Jesuits the idea that "the end justifies the means" — we quote the now proverbial version — for in fact they were careful to specify: "on condition that the means not be intrinsically vicious"; if this reservation were not sufficient, legitimate defense would not be possible.

an accidental lack of skill; such is the case of a person who is ill and not up to his task. Third: when there are valid reasons for supposing that the intention of a person well-known to be imperfect or bad was good in the given case; to be aware of it is to give evidence of a praiseworthy objectivity. Fourth: when the agent is substantially — not accidentally — incapable of executing his project in a satisfactory manner; such is the case of a child who tries to paint a picture, or of a crude or uncultivated man who tries to please with a gift in bad taste, but nonetheless honorable; in this case his intention as such is excused and not the deficiency affecting its expression; in the case of the child, even the deficiency is excused, if it is simply a question of age. Fifth, when an act or an extrinsically paradoxical, or even blameworthy, work is comprehensible only in the light of its spiritual intention; such is the case, for example, of certain erotic symbolisms which de jure and de facto refer to metaphysical or mystical realities, and which owing to their ambiguity pertain to the domain of esoterism.

But let us now return to ordinary intentions: one has to beware of arguing, merely in order to sentimentally excuse an author who after all is responsible for a blameworthy or even harmful work, that the work is acceptable because the intention was good; for that means that the defects of the work have a right to exist, and also that subjectivity has priority over objective reality; whereas "there is no right superior to that of the truth."

For example, one should not excuse a decadent and false art on the pretext that the intention of the artist was good since the content is religious; this would be to forget that the devil may wish to harm religion through believers who, as such, are obviously well-intentioned; thus it is not enough, in such cases, for the intention to be subjectively good, it must also be objectively so, that is, in its productions; the objective quality being one of the measures of the subjective quality, hence of the intention, for "ye shall know them by their fruits."[2] We have in mind here a necessary quality of a work, not merely a desirable one; the insufficiency of a work which is merely unskillful and naive, but innocent, is not of the same order as the badness of an ill-inspired work. Clearly, the falsity of an artistic or literary production can manifest a fundamental defect: a lack of self-knowledge, an unhealthy desire for originality, hence basically pride, whatever the superficial intention of the author. That the latter may believe that which is bad to be good and that his intention, on this basis, may be sincere, does not constitute an extenuating circumstance, otherwise one would have to excuse all errors and all crimes, as, by the way, is done all too readily in our day.

An intention may be good in one respect and bad in another: for example, it is good inasmuch as it manifests a religious sentiment, and it is bad inasmuch as it does so in a way that, strictly speaking, is incompatible with religion, holiness, dignity. To manifest a false, stupid or perverse mentality, is obviously to wish to do so; it is to identify with this mentality, and in this respect the intention could not be good. Spontaneous, hence sincere, originality may of course be justified; but the desire for originality is never justifiable. No doubt, the desire to make something new can kindle a talent, but it certainly lacks piety and also grandeur.

The fixed idea that the argument of intention is a panacea has become so habitual that too many people abuse it without reflecting, by protesting their good intention in cases where the question of intention could not even arise. Quite

---

2. In the religious painters of the *Quattrocento*, the intention concretely takes priority over the execution: we do not reproach a Fra Angelico for not having been a painter of icons, given his capacity to create a quasi-paradisal climate, thus sacralizing an art that strictly speaking was already profane. On the other hand, one must not overestimate the material and even the spiritual adequateness of certain icons, since they much more often express a collective religious sentiment rather than the full reality of the subject represented.

generally, it is all too clear that good intentions in no way constitute a guarantee of a man's worth, nor even, consequently, of his salvation; in this sense, intention is worthy only through its actualization.[3]

\*

\* \*

Intentionism and sincerism go hand-in-hand; what the first has in common with the second is that it flies to defend all things blameworthy, whether extravagant and pernicious or simply mediocre and vulgar; in short, to be "sincere," is to show oneself "as one is," unconditionally and cynically, hence counter to any effort to be what one ought to be. It is forgotten that the worth of sincerity lies in its contents only, and that it is charity to avoid giving a bad example; the individual owes society a correct comportment, to say the least, which has nothing to do with the vice of dissimulation. Let us specify that correct comportment, such as is required by good sense and traditional morality, has as a necessary corollary a certain effacement, whereas hypocrisy by definition is a kind of exhibitionism, crude or subtle as the case may be.

Still in connection with intentionism and sincerism, it is necessary to point out the common abuse of the word "understand," or of the notion of "understanding": we are told that one has to "understand" an evil-doer or a bad man and that to understand is to forgive. If this were so, what is one to think of sinners who convert, and above all of the traditional injunction to "know thyself"?[4] The good thief of

---

3. As the German — or the analogous English — proverb has it: "The road to hell is paved with good intentions" *(Der Weg zur Hölle ist mit guten Vorsätzen gepflastert);* doubtless they derive from this saying of Ecclesiasticus (21:10): "The way of sinners is smoothly paved with stones, but at its end is the pit of Hades." And according to the Epistle of Saint James (4:17), "To him that knoweth to do good, and doeth it not, to him it is sin."

4. Or "hate thy soul," according to a Christian formula.

the Gospel did not go to Paradise for nothing, and Saint Augustine knew what he was doing when writing his Confessions. With a quite characteristic inconsistency, the partisans of unconditional "understanding" — it is as if it sufficed to be "me" to always be right — are always careful to keep from "understanding" those who think otherwise, and whom they vilify shamelessly; a one-way charity necessarily ends in an upside-down justice.

Intention determines not only actions, but obviously also moral attitudes. There is a humility, a charity and a sincerity — but these are then merely appearances — stemming from hypocrisy, hence properly from satanism, namely: egalitarian and demagogic humility, humanistic and basically bitter charity, and cynical sincerity. There are false virtues whose motives are basically to demonstrate to oneself that one has no need of God; the sin of pride consists here in believing that our virtues are our property and not a gift of Heaven; which is all the more wrong in that, in this case, the virtues are imaginary, since pride perverts them.

To be sincere, and thus to have a good intention, means among other things that one take the trouble to reflect and also, when necessary, to inform oneself, above all when a serious matter is at issue; we cannot, when pleading a good intention, justify the error of someone who judges and concludes without making use of his intelligence and is heedless of what others think or know, even when they are better than he. There are people who, disdaining the religions and traditional wisdoms,[5] believe they can draw everything from within themselves, for which there is logically not the slightest reason; no doubt, the sage draws everything

---

5. It is arbitrary to object that the religions contradict each other, for one can also, and with even more reason, argue that they coincide in the essential and that their antinomies in no way diminish their intrinsic efficacy. To say religion, is to say revelation, whether primordial or historic; the pseudo-religions could not be efficacious, nor could methods removed from their traditional framework.

"from within himself" — *regnum Dei intra vos est* — in the sense that he benefits from intellectual intuition. But such intuition, aside from the fact that it has nothing to do with either ambition or, a fortiori, presumption, accords with the sacred traditions, from which the sage does not dream of turning away, even if he is born with infused knowledge. Be that as it may, religions and wisdoms are values as "natural" — although "supernaturally" so — as the air we breathe, the water we drink, the food we eat; not to acknowledge the "categorical imperative" of what by comparison we could term "spiritual ecology," is therefore an attitude as self-destructive as it is unrealistic.

*
* *

Still in connection with the questions of intention and sincerity, but in a very particular domain, let us now consider a quite important point in initiatory "alchemy": starting from the idea that the two poles of the contemplative path are mental concentration and intention of the heart, it will easily be understood why the latter has priority over the former; for it is obviously better to have the appropriate intention without knowing how to be well-concentrated than to know how to concentrate properly but without being concerned about the right intention.[6]

God listens to the intention of even the incapable, but He would not accept the technical perfection of the ambitious and the hypocritical. All this is said without losing sight of the fact that, in another respect, the quality of concentration depends upon the intention, precisely.

6. Metaphysical discernment first of all, then concentration that is sincere — because conforming to discernment — and quasi-permanent; this is the very foundation of operative spirituality, whatever might be its modes or degrees.

\*

\*  \*

Following these parenthetical remarks, let us redescend into the arena of current and "horizontal" psychology and say a few words concerning a notion that is abused scandalously in climates of psychoanalytical narcissism, namely that of "traumatism." In reality, man has the right to be legitimately traumatised only by monstrosities; he who is traumatised by less is himself a monster; the alternative is inexorable. Clearly, a traumatism has no right to be absolute; it is there to be overcome and to be assimilated in view of that which is the reason for being of our life and of our very existence. There is no worse hypocrite than an ungrateful and spiteful man who pretends to flee toward God; God cannot be loved out of hatred for one's fellow men. Many saints had good reasons for being "traumatised," but accepted the injustices — not imaginary in their case — "for the love of God," and without forgetting that "as thou hast done it shall be done unto thee."[7]

But one also has to consider the case of collective traumatism: it is natural for a people, or some large human group, to be traumatised without there being any reason to blame them therefore; and again, it is quite natural that this would not affect every individual. A collective soul is passive, and it is necessarily so since it can have neither a homogeneous intelligence nor the free and precise will that stems from it; this is one more reason not to allow oneself to be dominated by a collective psychism and not to let it come into power. Although passive, the collectivity can nonetheless be the vehicle of a good disposition, depending on its mental and moral health combined with the tradition; *vox populi, vox dei.*

7. A classic example is Saint John of the Cross, always persecuted and in the end canonized; but never "traumatised," to say the least.

Let us return now to the question of sincerity: it is not astonishing that to the sincerism in fashion, secrecy is something hateful, since, from that point of view, to be sincere is to hide nothing, and to hide something is to be dishonest or hypocritical. Now for obvious reasons, man has a natural right to secrecy: he has the right not to show a feeling or a fortiori a spiritual grace that concerns only himself;[8] a saint may wish to dissimulate, if not his virtues, at least his sanctity. Sincerity thus consists less in showing in every respect what one is, than in not wishing to appear to be more than one is — which a dignitary invested with a social or spiritual function could not be blamed for, since his normative demeanor refers to the principle he represents and not to his individuality. For the mentality of "our times" on the contrary, sincerity is vulgarity and vice versa, which presupposes the opinion that man is normally vulgar; thus vulgarity has become quasi-official. Moreover, dignity stems from piety, from awe as well as from love; even the sinner has the right to visible dignity, which is to say that dignity is incumbent upon him because he is a human being, "made in the image of God," despite his insufficiency or betrayal. To be sure, there are perverse men who affect worthy manners — impostors, for example — but they do so for false reasons, hence through hypocrisy; true dignity could not be affected, it is sincere by definition. Man is noble to the extent that he identifies with the principial and thus with the necessary; with the archetype and not with the accident.

From all that we have just said it follows that the man of "aristocratic" nature — we are not speaking of social classes — is he who masters himself and who loves to master himself;

8. "Neither cast ye your pearls before swine," Christ said.

the "plebeian" by nature — with the same reservation[9] —
is on the contrary he who does not master himself, and who
does not wish to do so. To master oneself is in substance to
want to transcend oneself, in conformity with the reason for
being of that central and total creature which is man; in fact,
the man of the "dark age" lives below himself. Thus he must
transcend himself — or reestablish the equilibrium between
*Māyā* and *Ātmā* — in accordance with a norm which he bears
within himself, and which comprises all that makes life worth
living.

Finally, the main question is to know what we are, or what
man is; now our true identity is in our consciousness of the
Real, of the Immutable, of the Sovereign Good. All psychological, moral, social and spiritual anthropology has to have
its foundation in this axiom; it follows that to defend man is
above all to defend him against himself.

*
* *

Returning now to our initial subject, we shall again specify,
at the risk of repeating ourselves, that intention essentially
comprises two dimensions, or that it operates in two times:
firstly, the good ought to be done, and secondly, it ought to
be well done. To accomplish a good is also to accomplish it
well, for the execution ought to be up to the idea; this is what
sincerity as well as logic demand. As we have seen above,
"right doing" also comprises, in principle if not always in
fact, formal language, or let us say the mode of expression
of the execution.

Another fundamental point is the accentuation, either of
the intention or of the action; an excessive legalism will see
in correct action a gauge of merit and virtue, whereas a

9. All the more so in that the social classes have become largely artificial
owing to destructive, dehumanizing and enslaving industrialism. The
phenomenon of aristocratic peasants and craftsmen, above all in countries
that are still fully religious, should be well known.

unitive mysticism[10] will readily see in outward observances a formalism that is either secondary or even superfluous; rightly or wrongly according to case, or according to the spiritual scope of the subject. In principle, the second attitude has priority over the first because the inward has priority over the outward, or because, precisely, intention has priority over action; but in this case the intention at issue is an intrinsic one, that is to say, sufficient unto itself and concretely encompassing the possibilities of meritorious action.[11] From Christ's standpoint, the observance of a prescription is obligatory only on the double condition that the prescription adequately express its reason for being and that man, in acting, realize this reason for being in his soul; as King David said (40: 6,8): "Sacrifice and offering thou didst not desire; mine ears hast thou opened . . . thy law is within my heart."

10. This expression should be understood in the widest sense, including gnosis as well as the way of love; *jnāna* as well as *bhakti*.

11. The distinction "intention-action" evokes the complementary relationship between "faith" and "works." The speculative and operative divergences that these two principles have given rise to in the East as well as in the West are well-known.

# Remarks on Charity

The word "charity" signifies goodness that makes itself known, goodness in action. Theologically, by charity is meant the love of God and neighbor; in ordinary language, the word charity, considered in isolation, means beneficial action in relation to those who need it; but in certain contexts, this word also means: to be considerate of others' feelings. Thus it is commonly said: "Out of charity, do not tell him that, it could make him sad," or: "Be good enough to please him in this way"; all of which has nothing to do with caring for the sick or with giving alms.

When charitableness is reproached for being accompanied by an "excessive indulgence" or "condescension," this reproach has in view merely a sentimental contingency that is difficult to measure and largely uncertain; for "let not thy left hand know what thy right hand doeth," and elementary virtue has always required that charity be done as modestly as possible. Thus it suffices to keep this in mind; and this has no connection with the concept as such of charity, seeing that charity itself requires that it be exercised charitably, hence modestly.

On the other hand, if he who receives feels humiliated or wounded by the obvious inequality that all charity comprises, it is very often because he is proud, and not because the benefactor manifests conceit. In our time of systematic and intensive demagoguery, one has to be sceptical with regard to gratuitous and hypersensitive protestations of

71

"human dignity." If the benefactor has to make an effort to be modest, the beneficiary of the good deed must in his turn make an effort not to be offended in an unseemly manner; virtue is needed on both sides! If it is necessary to "educate" someone, it is necessary to educate the poor man as well as the rich, above all when the fault of the former is more serious than that of the latter, which in our time is too frequently the case.

In charity there can be no "equal partners" since the one who helps or gives does so freely; if he does not do so freely, there is no charity. If someone collapses on the street, it is not an act of charity to help him; it is a human duty. Similarly, when someone suffers from hunger, it is a duty to feed him; but the degree of our help is a question of charity, for in this evaluation we are free. Each time there is a possible choice in the degree of our charitable intervention, there is freedom on our part and there is inequality between him who gives and him who receives; it is this which proves the duty of gratitude on the part of the latter.

What has to be eliminated is not the nature of things, that is, no natural element — material or psychological — of charity, but solely the sentimental abuses that have been blamed at all times. One has to beware of turning the beneficiary of charity into an insolent protestor, incapable of appreciating another's generosity; the man who does not know how to say "thank you" whole-heartedly, and without concerning himself with the psychology of his benefactor, is a monster.

Moreover, "partnerism" in charity coincides with the abolition of respect for all superiority; in a world in which each person believes himself to be the equal of everyone else in every respect, there is assuredly no place for free, hence generous and authentic, charity.[1]

---

1. We have heard it said that the traditional conception of charity is false because it implies a hierarchy, which is monstrous since hierarchy, and with it inequality, are to be found everywhere in the world and result from the very nature of Being.

# Remarks on Charity

\*

\* \*

We have been told that instead of relieving poverty, one has to teach men how to escape it; now, this aspect of charity is extremely limited, for the causes of poverty can be in the lack of technical skills; they can also be in the incapacity to manage money, or even in laziness; this is to say that they are moral as well as material. Besides, the meaning of the word "poverty" is quite relative, for in our day, the term is used for economic situations that are doubtless primitive, but in themselves altogether normal and satisfying, and it is done with the not very charitable underlying thought of finding new outlets for industrial products; wants are created in order to find buyers, and to find them it is necessary, on the one hand, to make real or fictitious poor people believe that the non-satisfaction of these wants is poverty and, on the other hand, to teach them what to do to make money. All of which is far from charity, whatever be the phraseology and the euphemisms; and which is even rather far, in too many cases, from efficacy and concrete good.

Charity is to freely, and really, help those who need and deserve it.

# No Initiative without Truth

At the beginning of this century, hardly anyone knew that the world is ill — authors like Guénon and Coomaraswamy were preaching in the desert — whereas nowadays, almost everyone knows it; but it is far from the case that everyone knows the roots of the evil and is able to discern the remedies. In our time one often hears that to fight against materialism, technocracy and pseudo-spiritualism, what is needed is a new ideology, capable of resisting all seductions and all assaults, and of galvanizing those of good will. Now, the need for an ideology, or the desire to oppose one ideology to another, is already an admission of weakness, and all initiatives stemming from this prejudice are false and doomed to fail. What must be done is to counter false ideologies with the truth that has always been and that we could never invent, since it exists outside us and above us. The present world is obsessed by the bias towards dynamism, as if it were a "categorical imperative" and a panacea, and as if dynamism were meaningful and efficacious outside truth pure and simple.[1]

1. In popular language this is called "putting the cart before the horse." We recall that during the Depression, one spoke of "creating a mystique of recovery"; as if the fatalities of industralism were imaginary maladies, curable through autosuggestion, and as if autosuggestion could transform subjective chimeras into objective realities.

No man in possession of his faculties could have the intention of substituting one error for another, whether "dynamic" or not; before speaking of strength and efficacy, one ought to speak of truth and nothing else. A truth is efficacious to the extent that we assimilate it; if it does not give us the strength we need, this merely proves we have not grasped it. It is not for the truth to be "dynamic," it is for us to be dynamic thanks to the truth. What is lacking in today's world is a penetrating and comprehensive knowledge of the nature of things; the fundamental truths are always accessible, but they could not be imposed on those who refuse to take them into consideration.

It goes without saying that what is in question here are not the altogether outward data with which experimental science can provide us, but realities that this science cannot handle, and which are transmitted to us by quite different channels, especially those of mythological and metaphysical symbolism, not to mention intellectual intuition, the possibility of which resides principally in every man. The symbolic language of the great traditions of mankind may seem difficult and disconcerting for certain minds, but it is nevertheless intelligible in the light of the orthodox commentaries; symbolism — it must be stressed — is a real and rigorous science, and nothing is more aberrant than to believe that its apparent naivety issues from a simplistic and "prelogical" mentality. This science, which we may term "sacred," cannot be adapted to the experimental method of the moderns; the domain of revelation, of symbolism, of pure intellection, obviously transcends the physical and psychic planes and thus is situated beyond the domain of methods termed scientific. If we believe that we cannot accept the language of traditional symbolism because it seems to us fantastic and arbitrary, this only shows that we have not yet understood this language and certainly not that we have gone beyond it.

It is rather convenient to claim, as is so speciously done in our day, that the religions have compromised themselves over the course of centuries and that their role has now ended. When one knows what a religion really consists of, one also knows that the religions cannot compromise themselves and that they are independant of human abuses; in fact, nothing men do has the power to affect the traditional doctrines, the symbols and rites, so long of course as human actions remain on their own level and do not attack sacred things. The fact that an individual may exploit religion in order to bolster up national or private interests in no wise affects religion as message and patrimony.

Tradition speaks to each man the language he can understand, provided he be willing to listen; this reservation is essential, for tradition, we repeat, cannot become bankrupt; it is rather of man's bankruptcy that one should speak, for it is he who has lost the intuition of the supernatural and the sense of the sacred. Man has allowed himself to be seduced by the discoveries and inventions of an illegitimately totalitarian science; that is, a science which does not recognize its own limits and for that reason is unaware of what lies beyond them. Fascinated by scientific phenomena as well as by the erroneous conclusions he draws from them, man has ended up being submerged by his own creations; he is not ready to realize that a traditional message is situated on an altogether different level, and how much more real this level is. Men let themselves be dazzled all the more easily since scientism gives them all the excuses they want to justify their attachment to the world of appearances and thus also their flight before the presence of the Absolute in any form.

\*

\* \*

Spinozist, deist, Kantian and Free-Masonic humanism intended to achieve a perfect man outside the truths which give the human phenomenon all its meaning.[2] As it was of

2. A humanism that we could term "pre-atheism" since it prepared the ground for, or opened the door to, atheism properly so called.

course necessary to replace one God by another, this false idealism gave rise to the abuse of intelligence characteristic of the 19th century, especially to scientism and with it industrialism; the latter in its turn brought about a new ideology, one equally flat and explosive, namely the paradoxically inhuman humanism that is Marxism. The internal contradiction of Marxism is that it wants to build a perfect humanity while destroying man; which is to say that militant atheists, more impassioned than realistic, wish to overlook that religion is so to speak an ecological question. Assuming that religion comprises an element of "opium" — not only "for the people" — this element is "ecologically" indispensable for the human psychism; in any case, its absence brings about incomparably worse abuses than its presence, for it is better to have good dreams than to have nightmares. Be that as it may, only religion, or spirituality, offers that integral meaning and happiness anchored in man's deiform nature without which life is neither intelligible nor worth living.

An easy argument against religions is the following: the religions and denominations contradict one another, hence they cannot all be right; consequently none is true. It is as if one were to say: every individual claims to be "I," hence they cannot all be right; consequently, no one is "I"; all of which amounts to asserting that there is but one single man to see the mountain and that the mountain has but a single side to be seen. Only traditional metaphysics does justice to the rigor of objectivity and to the rights of subjectivity; it alone is capable of explaining the unanimity of the sacred doctrines as well as their formal divergences.

"When the inferior man hears about the Tao, he laughs at it; it would not be the Tao if he did not laugh at it . . . The self-evidence of the Tao is taken for darkness." These words of Lao-Tsu are more timely than ever; no doubt errors and stupidities cannot but be as long as their altogether relative possibility has not been exhausted; but it is certainly not they that will have the final word.

## No Initiative without Truth

*

* *

A point that we would like to stress at the risk of repetition is this: one readily speaks of the duty of being useful to society, but one fails to ask whether this society is useful, that is to say whether it realizes man's, and thus a human community's, reason for being; quite clearly, if the individual must be useful to the collectivity, the latter for its part must be useful to the individual. The human quality implies that the collectivity could not be the aim and reason for being of the individual, but on the contrary that it is the individual, in his solitary station before the Absolute and thus by the exercise of his highest function, who is the aim and reason for being of the collectivity. Man, whether conceived in the plural or the singular, is like a "fragment of absoluteness" and is made for the Absolute; he has no other choice. The social can be defined in terms of the truth, but the truth cannot be defined in terms of the social.

These considerations lead us to the pointlessly controversial question of "altruism": there are "idealists," in India as in the West — which can be seen in the sentimentalism of a Vivekananda — who readily blame "those who seek their own salvation" instead of concerning themselves with saving others; an absurd alternative, for one of two things must hold true: either it is possible to save others, or it is impossible to do so; if it is possible, this implies that we first seek our personal salvation, otherwise saving others is impossible, precisely; in any case, it is no favor to anyone to remain attached to one's own faults. He who is capable of becoming a saint but neglects to become one cannot save anyone; it is hypocrisy pure and simple to hide one's own weakness and lukewarmness behind a screen of good works. Another error, related to the one just mentioned, consists in believing that contemplative spirituality is opposed to action or makes man incapable of acting; an opinion belied by all the Scriptures, particularly the *Bhagavad Gītā.*

79

\*

\* \*

No initiative outside the truth: this is the first principle of action, without, however, being a guarantee of success; still, man must do his duty without asking whether he will be victorious or not, for faithfulness to principles has its own intrinsic value, it bears its fruit in itself and means ipso facto a victory in the soul of the agent. We are in the "iron age," and outward victory can come about through a divine intervention alone; nonetheless, logically and spiritually correct activity can have incalculable effects, and in any case partial effects, outside us as well as within us.

# Being Conscious of the Real

The purpose of human intelligence, and consequently the purpose of man, is the consciousness of the Absolute, beyond but also within the consciousness of contingencies. If it is to seek distraction in futilities, or to lead an antlike existence, then it is not worth being born into the human state, and the phenomenon of human intelligence — reduced to a pointless luxury — would be inexplicable.

In connection with man's vocation, it is necessary to understand Saint Anselm's ontological argument correctly: it does not mean that the capacity to imagine no matter what proves the existence of the thing imagined; it means that the capacity to conceive God proves a spiritual scope that is explained only by the reality of God. According to the same Doctor, faith comes before knowledge *(credo ut intelligam);* in short, faith is here presented as the qualification for intellection, which is to say that in order to be able to understand, one has to possess the sense of the transcendent and of the sacred. But the inverse is also true: "I understand that I may believe" *(intelligo ut credam)* — which no one has ever said — could mean that before possessing a quasi-existential certitude of transcendent realities, it is important to grasp the doctrine. In a certain respect, the predisposition of the heart is the key to metaphysical truth reflected in the mind; in another respect, this conceptual knowledge is the key to the science of the heart.

"Blessed are they that have not seen, and yet have believed": it is a question here of the outer man, immersed in the maze of phenomena. Faith is the intuition of the transcendent; unbelief stems from the layer of ice that covers the heart and excludes this intuition. In mystical language, the human heart is either "liquid," or "hardened"; it has also been compared to a mirror that is either polished or rusted. "They that have believed": they who place the intuition of the supernatural above a way of reasoning that is servile and cut off from its roots.

\*

\*   \*

We have said that man's vocation is the consciousness of the Absolute; the parable of the persevering widow and the unjust judge reminds us that this consciousness, which is "now," ought to be "always," which is to say that its very content demands totality; it must be "always" lest it be "never." However, to "pray without ceasing," as Saint Paul wishes, could not imply a perfect continuity, unrealizable in earthly life; in fact, perseverance works through rhythms — rigorous or approximate — and it is these that serve as perpetuity. The inevitable gaps between spiritual acts are recipients of grace — the angels do for us what we cannot do — so that the life of prayer suffers no discontinuity.

Nothing gives us the right to forget the Essential; to be sure, our earthly existence is woven of pleasures and labors, joys and sorrows, hopes and fears, but all that is without common measure with the consciousness of the Absolute and with our quasi-ontological duty to practice it. "Let the dead bury their dead," said Christ, and he added: "And follow me"; namely, in the direction of the "kingdom of God which is within you."[1]

---

1. The same meaning is found in this saying: "But thou, when thou prayest, enter into thy closet, and when thou hast shut thy door, pray to

In order to be thus faithful to ourselves we have need of irrecusable arguments: keys allowing us to remain within the consciousness of the Sovereign Good despite the troubles of the world and of the soul. The fundamental argument is that *"Brahman is real, the world is illusory" (Brahma satyam jagan mithyā)*, which cuts short all the ruses of the earthly *māyā;* doubtless, this argument is intellectually and psychologically most demanding, given that it presupposes a concrete intuition of the Real and not merely an abstract idea; it must therefore be accompanied by other key ideas, closer to our earthly and daily experience.

On the plane of our human relationship with God, the first indispensable argument is the evidence that the world cannot be other than what it is and that we cannot change it; hence that we must resign ourselves to that which cannot but be, and resist all temptation to revolt — albeit unconscious — against destiny and against the nature of things; this is what is called "accepting the will of Heaven." To the quality of resignation is joined that of trust; the Divinity is substantially benevolent, its intrinsic goodness precedes its quasi-accidental rigor; to be conscious of this is to dwell in peace and to know that all things are in God's hands.

In many cases, it matters little that our right be safeguarded; egoism — or let us say, the bias of not being able to bear any injustice — is a serious pitfall in our relationship with Heaven, and that is why Christ prescribed loving one's enemies[2] and turning the left cheek. In a word, one has to know how to forget oneself before God and in view of our last ends, all the more so as in the final analysis it is only in this climate of detachment that we can have access to the

thy Father which is in secret. . . ." Similarly again: "No man, having put his hand to the plough, and looking back, is fit for the kingdom of God."
2. This is the condemnation, not of the defense of a vital right, but of excess in the defense of that right; justice is not vengeance.

certitude, both transcendent and immanent, that "the soul is not other than *Brahman*" *(jivo brahmaiva nāparah)*.[3]

To the qualities of resignation and trust ought to be joined that of gratitude: quite often, the remembrance of the good things we enjoy — and which others may not enjoy — can attenuate a trial and contribute to the serenity demanded by the consciousness of the Absolute. Another argument, finally, is based on our freedom: we are free to do what we want to do, to be what we want to be; no seduction or trial can prevent us from having recourse to the saving consciousness of the Sovereign Good.

\*

\*   \*

In our consciousness of God, our desire for liberation meets the will of God to free us; prayer is at once a question and a response. If "beauty is the splendor of the true," the same can be said of goodness; if the good tends to communicate itself, that is because it also tends to liberate us.

Christ's injunction to "love God with all thy heart, with all thy soul, with all thy strength and with all thy mind," reminds us that the consciousness of the Absolute is absolute: that we can know and love That which alone is only with all that we are. The unicity of the object demands the totality of the subject; this indicates that in the last analysis the object and the subject rejoin in pure Reality, which is at once the undifferentiated Essence and ultimate Cause, hence the Source of all differentiation. To say Absolute is to say Infinite, and in consequence manifestation and diversity; and the projection of the Good implies ontologically the return to the Good.

\*

\*   \*

3. A consciousness that on the one hand transcends the ego and on the other belongs to its transpersonal essence.

Discernment and contemplation; concentration and perseverance; resignation and trust; humility and charity. Spirituality is what man is: being made of intelligence, will and sentiment — all three faculties having the principial quality of objectivity on pain of not being human — spirituality has as its constitutive elements the Truth, the Way and Virtue; Virtue giving rise to the two complementary poles of humility and charity, precisely. The Way is attached to the Truth; Virtue is attached to both the Truth and the Way.

Humility prolongs — in moral mode — the element Truth or Knowledge, because Knowledge teaches us the proportions of things; man could not know metaphysical Reality without first knowing himself. Charity prolongs the element Way or Realization because this element essentially calls upon Grace; man could not deserve mercy without being merciful himself. He who unduly raises himself will be abased, and he who abases himself — in conformity with the nature of things — will be raised; and this through participation in the elevation of the Real. And similarly: he who unjustly rejects his neighbor will be rejected by God, and he who accepts his neighbor — in conformity with justice and generosity — will be accepted by God, by Him who is hidden in the "neighbor" in virtue of the omnipresence of the Self. It will have been understood that charity refers more particularly to immanence, and humility to transcendence.

A priori, metaphysics is abstract; but it would not be what it is if it did not give rise a posteriori to concrete prolongations on the plane of our human and earthly existence. The Real encompasses all that is; the consciousness of the Real implies all that we are.

# The Liberating Passage

From the standpoint of transcendence, there is quite evidently a discontinuity between the Divine Principle and its manifestation; but from the point of view of immanence, there is continuity. According to the first relationship, we shall say "manifestation and not Principle"; according to the second, "manifested Principle, hence still Principle." When there is discontinuity, we distinguish between the Essence and the form; when there is continuity, we distinguish between the Substance and the accident. In both cases, there is Reality and the veil; Absoluteness and relativity.

In order to be less abstract, let us specify that the accident is to the Substance what ice or steam is to water, and that the form is to the Essence what the reflection is to the sun; or again, on quite a different plane, the relationship between the participle and the verb equals that of the accident and the Substance, and the relationship between the word and the thing signified equals that between the form and the Essence. And similarly in the spiritual domain: when we distinguish between the symbol and its principial archetype, the "Idea" *(Eidos)*,[1] we refer to the discontinuous and static relationship "form-Essence"; but when we distinguish between the rite and its effect, we refer to the relationship

---

1. Or the "Paradigm," which is the Idea viewed in its aspect of initial Norm or celestial Ideal. We use capital letters when it is a question of the Divine Order, even though we fear overusing them.

"accident-Substance," which is continuous and dynamic. This is to say that the accident is a "mode" of the Substance, whereas the form is a "sign" of the Essence.[2]

Every sacred symbol is an "enlightening form" that invites to a "liberating rite"; the "form" reveals the Essence to us, whereas the "rite" leads us back to the Substance; to the Substance we are, the only one that is. All this concerns, on the one hand sacred art, "liturgy," and on the other hand the beauties of nature; it also concerns, with all the more reason, the symbolism of concepts and the rites of assimilation. Vision of the Essence through the form, and return to the Substance by means of the rite.

There is the visual symbol and the auditory symbol, then the acted symbol, all of which bring about the passage from the outward to the Inward, from the accident to the Substance, and thereby also the passage from the form to the Essence.[3] Let us take the opportunity here to point out that a noble and profound person tends to see the Substance in the accidents, whereas an inferior person sees only the accidents and tends to reduce the substantial manifestations to a trivializing accidentality. The sense of the sacred and of the celestial is the measure of human worth.[4]

*
* *

So, when confronting the notions of "form" and "essence," it will be said that there is discontinuity; when confronting the notions of "accident" and "substance," it

2. However, the terms "substance" and "essence" are synonymous inasmuch as they simply designate the archetypal content of a phenomenon.

3. In a particularly direct way, music and dance are supports for a passage — at whatever degree — from the accident to the Substance; and this is above all the meaning of rhythm. The same is true of sacred nudity and all contemplative recourse to virgin Nature, the primordial sanctuary.

4. Which cuts short the hasty and barbarous distinction between the "savage" and the "civilized."

will be said on the contrary that there is continuity. But when one considers on the one hand the conformation of the form to the essence and on the other the manifestation of the essence in the form, or when one considers — and this amounts in practice to the same thing — the conformation of the accident to the substance and the manifestation of the substance in the accident, the question of discontinuity or continuity does not arise. For conformation which is "ascending," as well as manifestation which is "descending," are altogether independent of the distinction in question.

The divine symbol, by definition, is paradoxically ambiguous: on the one hand it "is God" — that is its reason for being — and on the other, it "is not God" — that is its earthly materiality; it is "image" because it is manifestation and not Principle, and it is participating emanation and liberating sacrament because it is *Ātmā* in *Māyā*. The human body in itself — not in a given diminished form — is a symbol-sacrament because it is "made in the image of God"; that is why it is the object of love *par excellence;* not to the exclusion of the soul that dwells in it, but together with this soul, for the human body has its form only in virtue of the content for which it is made. The body invites to adoration by its very theomorphic form, and that is why it can be the vehicle of a celestial presence that in principle is salvific; but, as Plato suggests, this presence is accessible only to the contemplative soul not dominated by passion, and independently of the question of whether the person is an ascetic or is married. Sexuality does not mean animality, except in perverted, hence sub-human, man; in the properly human man, sexuality is determined by that which constitutes man's prerogative, as is attested, precisely, by the theomorphic form of his body.

And this leads us back to our distinction between the Essence and the Substance: the masculine pole refers to essentiality and to transcendence, and the feminine pole to substantiality and to immanence. The trajectory towards the

Sovereign Good — which is at once the Absolute and the Infinite — necessarily comprises modes that are so to speak masculine as well as feminine; a priori and grosso modo, Truth pertains to Rigor and to Justice, and the Path, to Gentleness and to Mercy. In loving woman, man essentially loves Infinitude and Goodness; woman, in loving man, essentially loves Absoluteness and Strength; the Universe being woven of geometry and musicality, of strength and beauty.

We have said above that Transcendence means discontinuity between the Principle and its manifestation, hence separation, and Immanence means continuity, hence union; thus it is that divine Virility, with the implacability of the nature of things, imposes upon us principles that derive from the Immutable, and that on the contrary divine Femininity, with all the freedom that Love disposes of, grants us the imponderable graces that bring about the miracle of Salvation.

# INDEX

# Index

poles of 14
purpose of 81
total 1
unitive vs. separative 6
Intention 5, 56, 61-66, 69-70
Intuition 11-13, 18, 66, 76-77, 82
Inwardness 32, 56-58
*Ishvara* 25, 50
Islam 2, 9, 41

*Jīvan-mukta* 56
*Jīvātmā* 31
*Jnāna* 8, 70

Kaaba 41
Kabbalah 3
Knowledge 7, 13-15, 25, 44, 63, 66, 76, 81, 85
Koran 3, 59
Krishna 20, 27, 41
*Kulturheros* 32

Lalla Yogishwari 22
Lao-Tsu 78
*Līlā* 35, 56
Love 8, 43, 45, 57, 89-90
and fear 25
and hate 6-7, 44
and personality 5
and virtue 11
of beauty 2-6, 9, 31
of God 2, 15, 24, 57, 67, 70
of the Sovereign Good 9
objects of 9
poles of 2
purpose of 7
self-love 30

Man, men 1-2, 9, 11-17, 19-23, 25-35, 40-41, 43, 45, 50, 52, 56, 58-59, 67-70, 77-79, 81-82, 85. *See also* Human being
Manifestation 19, 40, 51-52, 59, 80-90
Mary 30, 52. *See also* Blessed Virgin
Mask, masks 27-31, 35, 36. *See also* Veil
Matter 18, 22, 34-36, 46
*Māyā* 8, 19, 33, 49-50, 52, 83. *See also* *Ātmā*
and *Ātmā* *vii*, 20-21, 26, 39-40, 42, 48, 50, 69, 89
and contingency 46
and the Divine Order 23
and the personal God 17-18
and relativity 17, 48

and symbolism 22, 27
degrees of 38-40
Memory 11, 13
Mercy 2, 25, 30, 39, 90
Metaphysics *vii*, 78, 85
*Metatron* 3
Method 11, 26
Morality 28, 56, 64
Muhammad 8
Mystery 36, 38
Mysticism 70

Nature 17, 20
Nudity, sacred 22, 41, 88

Object, absolute 47
Objectivity 1, 14-16, 78
Opposites, opposition 8, 38-39
Outwardness 55-58

Paradise 4, 10, 26, 31, 46, 49, 65
Paradox 38
*Paramātmā* 25, 50
Pascal, Blaise 61
Passivitity 32, 48
Perfect, perfection 8, 31-32, 34, 40, 57
Person (divine) 25
Personality 3, 5, 36, 43
Piety 3-5, 7, 10, 68
Plato, Platonic 11, 24, 89
Pleasure 30-31
Pneumatic 27-28, 31, 56, 59
Possibility 18-19, 37, 39-40
Prayer *vii*, 33, 84
Pride 20, 65
Principle 3, 17, 19, 22, 24, 40, 48-49, 85, 89-90
Profane 32, 52, 63
Projection 17-21, 26, 52
Prototype 20, 33

Radiation, creative 17-18
Real 6-7, 25, 69, 83, 85
Reality 8, 37, 59
absolute 24
and beauty 44
and relativity 87
contingent 50
degrees of 23
metaphysical 85
objective 62
of God 81
pure 84
Supreme 13

93

The Transcendent Unity of Religions, *Faber and Faber, 1953*
Revised Edition, *Harper & Row, 1974*
*The Theosophical Publishing House, 1984*

Spiritual Perspectives and Human Facts, *Faber and Faber, 1954*
*Perennial Books, 1969*
New Translation, *Perennial Books, 1987*

Language of the Self, *Ganesh, 1959*

Gnosis: Divine Wisdom, *John Murray, 1959*
*Perennial Books, 1990*

Stations of Wisdom, *John Murray, 1961*
*Perennial Books, 1980*

Understanding Islam, *Allen and Unwin, 1963, 1965, 1976, 1979, 1981*
*Penguin Books, 1972*

Light on the Ancient Worlds, *Perennial Books, 1966*
*World Wisdom Books, 1984*

In the Tracks of Buddhism, *Allen and Unwin, 1968*
*Unwin-Hyman, 1989*

Dimensions of Islam, *Allen and Unwin, 1969*

Logic and Transcendence, *Harper and Row, 1975*
*Perennial Books, 1984*

Esoterism as Principle and as Way, *Perennial Books, 1981*

Castes and Races, *Perennial Books, 1981*

Sufism: Veil and Quintessence, *World Wisdom Books, 1981*

From the Divine to the Human, *World Wisdom Books, 1982*

Christianity/Islam: Essays on Esoteric Ecumenicism,
*World Wisdom Books, 1985*

The Essential Writings of Frithjof Schuon (S. H. Nasr, Ed.)
*Amity House, 1986*
*Element, 1991*

Survey of Metaphysics and Esoterism, *World Wisdom Books, 1986*

In the Face of the Absolute, *World Wisdom Books, 1989*

95

The Feathered Sun: Plains Indians in Art & Philosophy,
*World Wisdom Books, 1990*

To Have a Center, *World Wisdom Books, 1990*

Roots of the Human Condition, *World Wisdom Books, 1991*

Images of Primordial & Mystic Beauty:
Paintings by Frithjof Schuon,
*Abodes, 1992*

Echoes of Perennial Wisdom, *World Wisdom Books, 1992*